HOW TO
KEEP HOUSE

THE LOST ART OF BEING A MAN

HOW TO
KEEP HOUSE

SAM MARTIN

BLOOMSBURY

First published in Great Britain 2004
Bloomsbury Publishing Plc, 38 Soho Square, London W1D 3HB

Copyright © Elwin Street Limited, 2004

Produced by Elwin Street Limited
35 Charlotte Road
London EC2A 3PD
www.elwinstreet.com

Designed by Headcase Design
Illustrations by David Eaton

First printing, March 2004
10 9 8 7 6 5 4 3 2 1

A CIP catalogue record for this book is available from the British Library.

ISBN 0-7475-7402-2

Printed in Singapore

All papers used by Bloomsbury Publishing are natural, recyclable products made from wood grown in well-managed forests. The manufacturing processes conform to the environmental regulations of the country of origin.

Disclaimer: The publisher, author, and copyright holder disclaim any liability from any injury that may result from the use, proper or improper, of the information contained in this book. Please always consult an expert where necessary as we do not guarantee that the information contained herein is complete, safe, or accurate.

CONTENTS

INTRODUCTION

Let's face it: most men are slobs. During the excitement of some sporting event or another, we mindlessly spill beer on the furniture. Left to our own devices, dishes and pizza boxes pile up in the kitchen sink and washing the clothes means taking a pair of jeans to the cleaners once a fortnight. The reason for this behaviour isn't that we don't notice the beer-spilling or the hurricane-like mess in the kitchen. It's just that we don't care. At least so long as it doesn't affect our health; or our sex lives; or how much money we earn.

Sadly, it's been that way for a long, long time – certainly as far back as the 1960s: that's when men started getting in touch with their feminine sides and women stopped cleaning up after them. You'd think such a dramatic change would have taught more men how to cook or clean house, but the fact is most men were left in the lurch by the women's movement. They were handed a box of detergent and a frying pan and that was it.

Curiously, a close look at the clothes-washing trends of the 1970s reveals an unexplained epidemic of shrunken, discoloured and generally ruined clothes sweeping across the nation. Also, restaurants in all the major cities began reporting significant increases in the number of take-away meals they were preparing each year. Is it coincidence that home delivery became big business in the 1980s and still is today? I think not. Men were just answering the new challenge in the best way they knew how: by being resourceful.

These days, however, things have changed. More and more men want to be in touch with their manliness (sales of power tools have been on the upswing since the start of the new millennium) and women will no longer tolerate men who can't organize themselves enough to wear a clean shirt and keep the bathroom smelling fresh. Unfortunately, having shunned manly work for almost an entire generation, most guys can't tell a hammer from a halibut and certainly couldn't manage to wash and iron a dress shirt if the Queen herself was knocking at the door. But that's because most guys haven't worked out that a well organized, well maintained and clean house will make them more popular, can improve their sex lives and can even make them rich.

It is not for nothing that homosexual men have become all the rage. They look good and always have jobs that pay them well. That's because they are organized, have great apartments and know how to iron a shirt. Fact is, homosexual men have great love lives, have no shortage of friends and throw great parties because they have hip furniture, fabulous kitchen appliances and (here's the clincher) clean bathrooms. So think *Queer Eye for the Straight Guy* and get yourself updated.

Believe me, it is possible for you to get organized, clean up your pad, look manly and learn some home-maintenance tips on the way – and it's all in this book. You'll find a section on clearing away clutter and creating better storage. All the cleaning basics are here, too, from how to swab out the bathroom before your date comes over to how to wash, dry and fold your clothes without shrinking them to the size of a postage stamp. You'll also learn about home repairs and the tools you'll need to get the job done – the stuff of manly lore the world over.

So if you're one of those guys still holding on to your messy ways, for the sake of your health, your love life and your well-being, it might be time to get yourself together and give you and your home an upgrade. It won't be pretty at first, there's no denying that. You'll be sorting through mountains of junk and embarking on a long list of repairs. But, make no mistake, in the end you'll be a better man for it.

GETTING
ORGANIZED

Even the most Zen-like among us will get red in the face and kick something if we can't find our tools. Then, during the ensuing search-and-destroy mission, things get worse: time ticks by; wives and girlfriends go unattended; steaks burn on the grill; and we miss important meetings with friends at the pub. It is galling to think it can all be avoided with just a little organization …

KEEPING CLUTTER
TO A MINIMUM

Some say that clearing clutter at home or at the office is one of the best exercises for clearing your mind (which will come in handy when you come to tackle some of the building projects in this book). It'll also simplify the space you live or work in, making your life feel less hectic and leaving you more in control.

You will need	**W H A T T O D O**
a routine	**1** Designate a "place" for everything in your house so that you know where to put stuff when it starts to pile up. Papers and bills should go in clearly labelled files. Dirty clothes should go in the laundry basket. Old newspapers and magazines should go in recycling bins.
somewhere to put everything	
bin bags	
the will to simplify your life	**2** After you use something – a book, a shirt, a pint glass – put it in its "place" instead of setting it down on the nearest table or chair, where it could end up staying for days.
	3 Develop a routine for cleaning around the house. A quick walk-through of each room at the end of the day, picking up and putting away,is a good way to keep clutter at bay.
	4 Have a convenient spot near the front door where you can keep your keys, wallet, spare change and sunglasses – things that are always impossible to find when you need them.
	5 Get into the habit of throwing stuff away.

STRATEGIES FOR STAYING ORGANIZED

Getting all your ducks lined up neatly in a row is one thing. Keeping them that way is quite another. For a man to keep the clutter permanently at bay and his life in a perpetual state of calm, he needs a plan.

WHAT TO DO

1. Devise a detailed routine and stick to it. Start every day by making your bed, and end every day by picking up clutter: the stuff in between will fall into place a little easier.

2. If the house, work, family and free time are overwhelming you into a state of paralysis, making organization seem out of the question, take one thing at a time. Focus on one room of the house and sort it. When that's done, move to the next room and so on.

3. Write yourself to-do lists. They can help clear your mind of worry and give you a visual aid for getting things done. Plus, as any woman will tell you, it's surprisingly satisfying to cross through an item on the list.

4. It may be easier said than done, but put everything back in its place immediately after you use it.

5. Wash the dishes after each meal.

6. Always be aware of what can be organized or categorized better. If you have just one desk drawer for pens, envelopes, paper clips and a hundred other office supplies, consider investing in some drawer dividers.

7. Always try to cut down on the things you need. How many back copies of *Car* magazine do you ever really look at?

ORGANIZATIONAL TOOLS

Getting organized is as much about being able to find a phone number, remembering a birthday or getting to meetings on time as it is about clearing away clutter and setting up a good routine. That's why a man is doomed without electronic gadgetry.

HAND-HELD DEVICES

If you keep missing important dates or can't keep up with your address book, a palmtop can help. These minicomputers are known variously as PDAs, palmtops or pocket PCs and have the ability to store thousands of addresses, log years' worth of dates, and give you wireless Internet access so that you can manage the household on the go. Some even have built-in global positioning systems and cell phones so that you'll never, ever get lost.

WHAT TO DO

1. If you simply need a palmtop to log important dates, and to keep phone numbers and to-do lists, you probably only need to spend a small amount of money on one with 8 megabytes of memory.

2. Pay attention to the battery life. Some may have to be charged more than others. Also, some will have removable batteries that you can replace once they wear out while others have built-in batteries that you're stuck with.

3. Go for the black-and-white screen unless you plan to watch videos on your palmtop. Then get glasses.

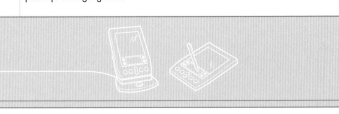

COMPUTERS

Before you go out and hand over a pile of money for a top-of-the-line computer, have an idea of what you plan to use it for. If it's going to help balance your chequebook, store email addresses and devise a glorified cleaning schedule, then you should opt for one with good Internet access, an accounting program and Microsoft Word, rather than one with a load of graphics software bundled into the deal.

WHAT TO DO

1. Decide whether you want a laptop or a desktop. Laptops are smaller and won't take up valuable room (ideal for reducing clutter). Desktops can be much easier to use, with larger keyboards, bigger monitors and a host of added accessories.

2. If you do go for the laptop, plan on buying a standard mouse to plug into it because most of the built-in ones suck.

3. If you're likely to be using the Internet regularly, consider spending the little extra cash it takes to get a high-speed connection. Otherwise it will take you forty-five minutes to find out if the weather is going to be fine enough for mowing the lawn at the weekend.

4. Also, don't skimp on the monitor. As with many things, bigger is better for laptops and desktops.

TIP

☑ You don't have to resort to electronic gadgetry: you'd be surprised how useful the age-old to-do list can be: write the task, do the task, cross out the task. One place to have a to-do list is on a chalk board that you can hang in the kitchen or some other central location. This is especially helpful if you've created your list with someone else and need to separate out the chores but track the progress of tasks that aren't yours.

TOP FIVE STORAGE IDEAS

When it comes to being organized you're not going to get far without storage space. This means you'll need to put every corner of your house to use (and make it look good in the process). That's where shelves, racks, cabinets, drawers and crates come in.

WHAT ARE THE OPTIONS?

1. Built-in or freestanding shelves are indispensable. They can be installed in any shape or size, anywhere in the house or garage, and can be anything from a single shelf in the bathroom to whole wall units in the living room (see page 84). Plus, they don't have to be fancy to be effective.

2. Racks and hooks are other simple storage options, and are often overlooked. If you have bikes or exercise equipment that are always getting knocked over, run into or stepped on, wall-mounted hooks or freestanding racks can help you get those toys off the ground. In the kitchen, hang some hooks to put pots and pans within easy reach.

3. Perhaps the best way to get your stuff out the way and out of sight is to add in a few cabinets, which are really just simple boxes with doors added to the front. The kitchen is where we're most used to cabinets but they can be installed anywhere – add a set in the bathroom for storing towels, for example.

4. Drawers are another fine place to stash your stuff and if you're going to add cabinets, why not equip them with a row of pull-outs (see page 83)? Drawers can be deep and wide to hold pots, pans, recycling containers, art supplies and clothes, or they can be small and thin to hold photographs, nails, tools and office supplies.

5. Too busy/lazy for do-it-yourself? Just go out and buy some good-looking boxes or crates. These can be made of wicker, wood or plastic and can be piled in a wardrobe, slid under the bed, or turned on their sides and stacked up to make a system of handy cubby holes. If you really don't want to spend a lot of money or time building shelves and drawers, this is the option for you.

KITCHEN BASICS

Every kitchen needs to be well equipped for everyday cooking and occasional entertaining. Once you've put the kitchen in order, it may become increasingly clear that it's time to upgrade or restock some of the basic kitchen gadgets, just in case you want to throw a party, or even cook dinner.

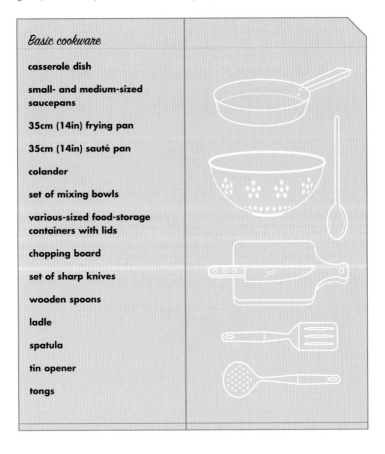

Basic cookware

casserole dish

small- and medium-sized saucepans

35cm (14in) frying pan

35cm (14in) sauté pan

colander

set of mixing bowls

various-sized food-storage containers with lids

chopping board

set of sharp knives

wooden spoons

ladle

spatula

tin opener

tongs

toaster

kettle

tea/coffee pot

cheese grater

teatowels

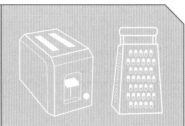

For entertaining

several dishes of varying sizes

serving spoons and forks

water jug

(in sets of eight):

cocktail glasses

tall water glasses

wine glasses

pint glasses/beer mugs

steak knives

**knives, forks, teaspoons,
soupspoons, tablespoons**

dinner plates

bread plates

small bowls

large bowls

coffee and tea mugs

ORGANIZING THE WARDROBE

All wardrobes have a limited amount of space in which to fit an inordinate amount of stuff. The two obvious flaws in a badly organized wardrobe are that, firstly, it takes an hour of digging and lifting things out of the way to find what you are looking for and, secondly, once you have it and try to pull it free, the entire contents of the wardrobe come with it, landing in a heap at your feet. Say goodbye to all this heartache.

You will need	**WHAT TO DO**
bin bags	1. Go through each item of clothing in your wardrobe and get rid of everything you haven't worn in the last year.
wooden coat hangers	
drawers and shelves	2. Replace flimsy and easily tangled wire coat hangers with sturdy wooden ones and take the throwaways to your local dry-cleaners for recycling.
crates	3. Once you thin out your hanging clothes, you may have enough room to put in a cabinet and set of drawers from floor to ceiling. Either that or you can stack up a number of wooden or plastic crates to create cubby holes for folded clothes and shoes.
tie hangers	
shoe racks	
	4. Separate clothes according to season and keep the appropriate set of clothes within easy reach in the wardrobe. Store the others in cabinets in the garage.

continued on next page

continued

5 Hang clothes according to type: trousers go together, then shirts, then suits. That way, everything is always easy to find. It's also helpful (and fun) to organize your shirts by colour.

6 Hang all ties and belts separately. Many shops sell tie racks that attach to the backs of wardrobe doors or fit over coat hangers.

7 Move your shoes off the floor and put them either in crates (see opposite) or in shoe racks, which come in many different designs. My favourite is the kind you hang on the back of the wardrobe door.

ORGANIZING A LINEN CUPBOARD

There are a number of reasons why you might be driven to get your house or flat in order (a lost lottery ticket or misplaced phone number come to mind right away) but, more often than not, a guy will vow to clean up because there's a woman on her way over, either for dinner or for good. If it's the latter, and you're going to be sharing the shower and the bedroom (stay focused here), then you're going to need more than just the one towel and the single set of bed sheets you've had since leaving home.

First off, you'll need hand towels (a woman won't want to dry her face on the towel you've dried your backside on), at least three more full-sized bath towels, at least three separate sets of sheets and pillowcases, a few more blankets (women get cold easily) and some tablecloths and linen napkins (for when the in-laws visit). You'll also need somewhere to keep it all.

WHAT TO DO

1. Group all like things together, with the bath towels in the easiest place to reach.

2. Swimming towels and blankets can be stored out of the way unless you go to the gym often (be honest) or live in a place where it's perpetually cold.

3. Sheets are used less often than towels but they still need to be more accessible than blankets or extra pillows, which you can also store in a linen cupboard.

4. Always fold towels and sheets in as flat a way as possible: they'll stack on top of each other more easily and you'll double the amount you can get in.

5. Place linen napkins near tablecloths, though if you have a dining-room dresser or an extra drawer in the kitchen, it makes sense to put them closer to the action.

STOCKING THE
BATHROOM CABINET

Stock your bathroom cabinet with plenty of minor first-aid stuff for treating headaches, muscle aches and most definitely heartburn. Of course, you'll also need some basic toiletries in there a) to give yourself a clean, decent appearance and b) to give yourself the appearance of having a clean, decent appearance. The latter is important if you happen to have a "guest" staying over. Plus, you'll be a hero if you keep an extra toothbrush around for her to freshen her breath in the morning.

You will need

anti-acid pills	hydrogen peroxide
nose- and ear-hair clippers	eye drops
thermometer	cotton balls
aspirin	cotton buds
lip balm	extra toothbrush
tiger balm	deodorant
dental floss	brush or comb
antibiotic cream	some kind of hair stuff, either mousse, gel or spray
plasters	
nail clippers	bar of soap
tweezers	extra razors
rubbing alcohol	extra shaving cream
	extra toothpaste

BASIC FIRST-AID KIT

Getting organized is tough business, especially when you're building shelves or replacing a broken window pane. As always, have a good first-aid kit around and pay attention to general safety rules.

Keep the kit in a handy place, such as in a linen cupboard or somewhere in the kitchen. Also, if you're doing a lot of work out in the garage, it's not a bad idea to stash a mini first-aid kit close by. As your wife or girlfriend may have already pointed out to you, it's not a good idea to run about the house covered in garage dirt (or blood).

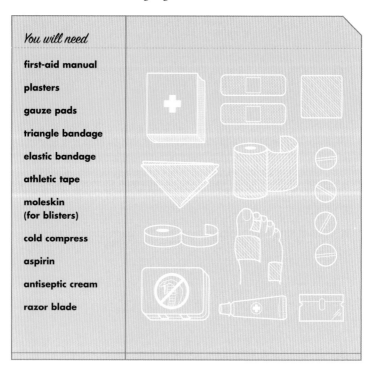

You will need

first-aid manual

plasters

gauze pads

triangle bandage

elastic bandage

athletic tape

moleskin (for blisters)

cold compress

aspirin

antiseptic cream

razor blade

GENERAL SAFETY TIPS

Picking up from the floor and arranging things in the house means a good deal of bending over combined with plenty of open cabinet and pantry doors. Be aware of all open doors and avoid whacking your head when you stand up because nothing will take the wind out of your organizational sail like a sharp blow to the skull.

Whenever you're working with wood, whether you're cutting it with a power saw or smoothing it down with sandpaper, always wear eye protection. You never know when a small sliver is going to lodge itself under your eyelid. If you're using loud power tools or vacuums, make sure you wear ear protection too.

Lifting heavy boxes, crates or furniture should not be treated lightly! Always squat down, keeping your upper body straight, and use your legs to lift, not your back. It'll prevent some extraordinary pain as well as having to lie flat on your back for two weeks.

CLEANING THE GARAGE

When the time comes to get a house in order, nothing strikes more fear into a man's heart than the notion of cleaning the garage. Years' worth of stuff can pile up in there and will typically include stacks of do-it-yourself manuals, projects that never materialized, old tennis shoes, broken garden tools – you name it. Often, garages can get so packed with junk that you can't even get the car in any more. If this sounds like your setup, it's time to get your hands dirty – you know it makes sense.

You will need	**WHAT TO DO**
a plan	1 The first thing a man should do in any dire predicament is assess the situation. Mentally divide the garage into four or five smaller areas and concentrate on one at a time.
plastic sacks or bin bags	
a garage sale	2 Divide what you find into three piles: garage-sale potential, rubbish and keep.
shelves, cabinets, hooks and drawers	3 Have a garage sale on a Saturday. This is a great way to make some money and meet pretty, if thrifty, girls. Invite friends to sell their own stuff and make a party of it with some music and beer. Be sure to make signs to announce your sale around the neighbourhood and don't get greedy by charging too much cash for your junk. The idea is to get rid of it.
broom	
scrubbing brush	
oven cleaner	
several dedicated days	
	4 Sort the stuff you don't want (and there will be plenty of it) into recycling, rubbish or things you can donate to charity.
	continued on next page

continued

5 Anything you want to keep should be organized according to its use (e.g. all garden tools should go in one place, sports equipment in another). Consider adding shelves, cabinets and drawers to get stuff off the floor and store it in an orderly way (see Top Five Storage Ideas, page 14). This is especially important for your tools, which can be hung efficiently on hooks attached to a piece of pegboard over your workbench. Sports gear can get put into large net bags, suspended from hooks, or stored on metal utility shelves.

6 Once you've thrown away, put away or sold the things in your garage it's time to sweep up the dust and get rid of the cobwebs. Give the floor a good scrub to finish off, using oven cleaner to remove persistent oil stains.

DO'S AND DON'TS

☑ Do decide the fate of every tiny scrap of paper, shred of material and useless knick-knack.

☒ Don't build or place shelves, cabinets or racks so that the car can't get in or the doors to the parked car can't open.

☒ Don't get sentimental about your junk. If a tattered old chair that you've been meaning to refurbish has been in the garage for more than three years, get rid of it.

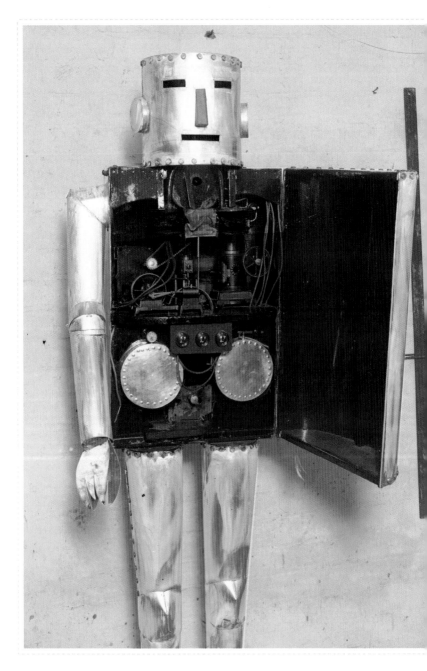

2

MACHINE MAINTENANCE

Appliances are only convenient for as long as they work and, alas, many times they don't. On the one hand this can be a great way for a man to use a few power tools but it can be a real pain in the neck as well. Either way, knowing what to do when the dishwasher gives up after a margarita party will win you many friends (and possibly job offers), even if all you do is come to the conclusion that the machine is unfixable and should be replaced … women like a man who takes control.

HOW MACHINES WORK AND WHAT TO DO IF THEY DON'T

Unless you cook your meat over an open fire, wash your underwear by hand and keep your beer cold in a spring-fed stream, you're going to need a few appliances. And, like any self-respecting man, you'll want to know exactly what you're getting into when you're taking on a microwave, tumble dryer or vacuum cleaner.

Appliances work through a combination of mechanics together with electricity or gas. Before you start dismantling your washing machine, it's very helpful to know how electricity works inside the house. It also helps to have a voltmeter on hand. You can use this simple and inexpensive tool to check whether an appliance is receiving power (or not), and this can save you a lot of time and trouble, especially if all you have to do is replace the power cord.

These days, most appliances are well made and trouble-free, but if you do happen to be lumbered with one that breaks down, it can usually be fixed without much effort. You will not need a PhD in rocket science, but the owner's manual is a must. That said, we men are resourceful beasts and, in some cases, the most resourceful thing you can do is call a professional, especially if your do-it-yourself handiwork is likely to put the gadget permanently out of order.

BASIC ELECTRICITY

When you're working on an electrical appliance it is always very important to disconnect the power before you lift a screwdriver. Thousands of volts of electricity pumping through your body is not good for your hair (or your long-term health).

Basically, electric power enters a house through two or three main lines that deliver about 240 volts of electricity to the various plug sockets, light switches and appliances in the house. This power is routed first into an electric meter outside the house, where it is measured (in amperes, or amps) and then into a circuit-breaker box or fuse box inside the house, where it is divided up into circuits to feed the various rooms and appliances. One room's plug sockets might be on one circuit, for example, while a big appliance, like the cooker, will have a circuit of its own.

Appliances can stop working if a circuit is overloaded (for example, if too many appliances are using one circuit) or if there is a short circuit somewhere in your wiring, or in the cord of the appliance itself (these can be dangerous and are recognizable as a burn or exposed wire).

If a circuit is overloaded, the circuit's fuse or breaker located in the breaker box will instantly cut off electricity to that circuit. Resetting a circuit breaker is as easy as flipping a switch inside the box, while a blown fuse has to be replaced. Once it is replaced, you have to make sure not to overload the circuit again.

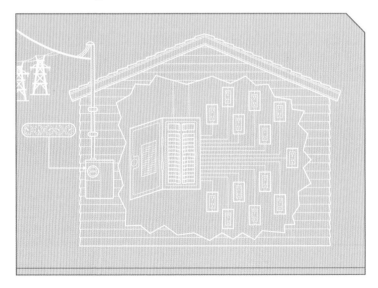

THE DISHWASHER

Regardless of what your mother says, if the dishes in a dishwasher don't get as sparkling clean as they should, that doesn't always mean you have to start rinsing more. It could be that the washer's timer isn't working properly so that the soap dispenser doesn't open, or that the water-inlet valve is broken, or that the tubing is clogged, preventing the machine from getting enough water.

You will need	**H O W T O**
owner's manual	**1** If the soap dispenser isn't opening, it will still be closed after the dishwashing cycle is finished. If this is the case, it usually means the timer assembly has malfunctioned and it needs to be replaced.
screwdriver	
new timer assembly	
new water-inlet valve	**2** Disconnect the dishwasher's electrical plug, or turn off the electricity to the dishwasher at your house's fuse box.
	3 The box-like timer assembly is located behind the timer knob on the control panel of the dishwasher. Refer to your owner's manual and remove the timer knob and dial.
	4 Locate the screws that hold the control panel to the dishwasher cabinet and remove the panel.
	5 The timer assembly should be screwed to the cabinet as well as attached to a set of wires. Unscrew the timer and unplug any wires (see Fig. A).

continued on next page

continued

6. Replace the old timer with a new one by following the above instructions in reverse.

7. If the soap dispenser is working properly and dishes are still coming out dirty, check to see that there's enough water getting into the dishwasher. If not, find the water-inlet valve by referencing your owner's manual.

8. If the valve is cracked or if there are rusty screws or water stains on the valve, it will have to be replaced.

9. Disconnect the dishwasher's electrical plug, or turn off the electricity at your fuse box, and turn off the water supply.

10. Remove the plumbing hose and the hose clamp that runs into the valve as well as the screws that hold the valve to the dishwasher cabinet (see Fig. B).

11. While the hose is off the inlet valve, check for any corrosion or blockages. Tap your screwdriver along the hose to loosen anything that might be crusted inside it, then hold the hose over a bucket and turn the water supply on to flush it out.

12. After turning the water back off, replace the old inlet valve with a new one.

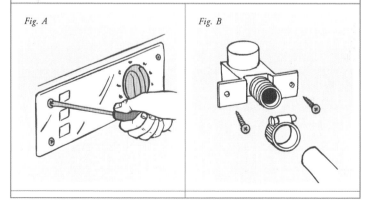

Fig. A

Fig. B

REPAIRING A WASHING MACHINE

Of all the appliances in the house, the washing machine is the one you least want to break down. Who wants to have to slog down to the laundrette once a week or, Heaven forbid, resort to wearing dirty clothes? As with most machines that break, there's a good chance the problem is an easy one to fix.

You will need	**H O W T O**
small bucket	**1** If the washing machine won't drain, see that the drainage hose isn't kinked, bent or blocked in a way that prevents water from passing.
screwdriver	
owner's manual	**2** Bail out as much water as you can into a nearby sink or bathtub using a small bucket.
	3 Use a screwdriver to unhook the hose from the machine, making sure you plan for all the water that's going to spill out when you do. Remove anything that could be clogging the hose.
	4 If the hose is clear, something could be blocking the pump, in which case refer to the owner's manual and find the pump.
	5 If the machine won't fill up with water, check for anything that might be stuck in the fill hose. If that's clear and the hose isn't kinked, remove the hoses to get at the screen filters inside the valves at the back of the washer.
	6 Don't remove the cone-shaped screens, but do clean them of any dirt or grime.

FIXING THE TUMBLE DRYER

If your dryer is squeaking and banging around, it means the machine is too damn old and you should get a new, fancy unit that can get your clothes wrinkle-free and mix a martini at the same time. Then again, it could mean the drive belt is loose, which is an easy fix.

You will need	**H O W T O**
owner's manual	**1** Disconnect the power to the dryer.
screwdriver	**2** Locate the screws that hold the dryer's top panel in place and remove the panel. Do the same for the front panel and the toe plate, if there is one.
new drive belt	**3** You should be able to see the drum: the belt fits around it and is connected to a motor attached to the bottom of the dryer case.
	4 Remove the loose or broken belt, taking time to note how and where it is fixed.
	5 Place a new drive belt around the cylinder (the grooves on the belt should face down) and thread it in place.
	6 Screw the toe plate and front and top panels back in place.

H I N T

☑ Sometimes big problems have easy fixes. If your dryer doesn't seem to be working as well as it should, it could be that it's not venting properly. Check the vent to make sure it isn't clogged or that the vent tube isn't kinked.

UNCLOGGING A GAS COOKER

If you're planning on cooking any romantic dinners at your place in the near future, make sure the hob is clean and that all the burners light. In gas hobs, dirt and grease build-up can block the gas and air needed to fuel the unit's burners.

You will need	**H O W T O**
paper clip **warm soapy water** **nailbrush**	**1** To repair burners that aren't lighting or are only lighting partially, prop up the hob rack to access the burners themselves, along with the burner tubes and the flash tubes. (The burner tubes supply the burners with air and gas and the flash tubes ignite the air and gas coming into the burner with the help of a pilot light or electric spark. The pilot or the electric-spark ignitor is located between the burners at the end of the short straight flash tubes.)
	2 Use a straightened paper clip to clean grease and dirt out of the tiny holes on the side of the burner nearest the flash tube so that gas can flow freely.
	3 If that doesn't do the trick, remove the burner and burner tube from the cooker by lifting the burner off its support and pulling the rigid tube off its valve (located behind the knob on the hob's control panel). You shouldn't need to unscrew any screws to do this.

continued on next page

continued

4 Soak the burner and burner tube in hot, soapy water before scrubbing them clean of any grime with a nailbrush.

5 Using a paper clip, ream out the flame openings found around the top edge of the burner.

6 Once the burner and tube have dried completely, put them back in place on the hob.

DO'S AND DON'TS

✓ Do ventilate the room if you smell gas when you're working on a gas hob.

✗ Don't light anything if there's a strong smell of gas in the room.

THE MICROWAVE

If the fan is whirring and the light is on inside your microwave but you're not getting enough heat to cook dinner, it is likely that you'll have to replace the high-voltage transformer (also called a plate transformer, a power transformer or simply a transformer). As usual, unplug this baby before you start unscrewing anything and, if in doubt, call a pro.

You will need	**WHAT TO DO**
owner's manual	1 Turn off the main power source to the microwave.
screwdriver with insulated handle	2 Locate the capacitor, usually found behind the side panel next to the control panel.
new transformer	3 Discharge it by touching the tip of an insulated-handle screwdriver simultaneously to both terminals. You should hear a "pop" when you do this.
	4 Disconnect all electrical wires going into the transformer (there should be four: two input wires and two output wires).
	5 Unscrew the mounting screws that hold the transformer to the body of the microwave.
	6 Screw in the new transformer and reconnect the wires to it in the same way they were connected to the old transformer.

DO'S AND DON'TS

☑   If there are three terminals on the capacitor, be sure to touch all three at the same time.

HOW TO DEFROST A FRIDGE-FREEZER

From time to time, the freezer at the top of your fridge will build up so much ice inside that the important stuff will start to get crowded out. Here's how to defrost the box and sluice out the fridge in one sitting.

You will need	**WHAT TO DO**
cool box	**1** Remove all food from the fridge-freezer and put it in a cool box. Turn the fridge thermostat off.
metal pot small enough to fit in the freezer	**2** Boil some water in a kettle and fill the small metal pot. Place the pot in the freezer.
kettle	**3** Place a towel on the floor in front of the fridge door to soak up water as it melts.
boiling water	**4** Fill the metal pot with fresh-boiled water each time it cools. After 3 hours you will be able to pull large chunks of ice away from the sides of the fridge.
towels	
sponge	**5** Once all the ice is gone, give the fridge a good clean with a sponge and soapy water.
about 7 hours	**6** Turn the fridge back on and close the door. It should be ready to keep food cold in 2 hours.

DO'S AND DON'TS

☒ If you're going to pry ice off, don't use a sharp knife, ice pick or anything else that could puncture the freezer walls and cause antifreeze to leak into the box.

VACUUM CLEANER

You'll know the vacuum cleaner needs some attention when you catch a whiff of the engine overheating, a terrible stench that smells like burning hair mixed with plastic. That usually means the belt needs changing – a common and easy fix – and the sooner you do it, the less damage will be done to the engine. If the machine doesn't turn on at all, check the connection and make sure you haven't blown a fuse. If it won't suck properly there are a few things that might do the trick.

WHAT TO DO

1. If the vacuum cleaner isn't sucking properly it may just need a couple of minor adjustments. If an electrical cord is frayed and not connecting properly, re-splice the wires together and patch the splice with plenty of electrical tape.

2. Check that the hose doesn't have any holes in it. If it does, wrap the hose and the holes with more electrical tape.

3. Change over-stuffed dust bags or clogged filters. They tend to inhibit the machine's sucking mechanism.

4. Check that the round, spinning brush thing under the vacuum – technically an agitator – is, in fact, spinning. If not, the rubber belt attached to it may be broken or there might be hair or string wrapped around the agitator, preventing it from doing its job. This can eventually burn out an engine.

5. Some vacuums with agitators and brushes need to be adjusted so that they are an appropriate height off the carpet. Too close, and the sucking mechanism is effectively smothered.

6. For vacuum cleaners with a tube, make sure there isn't anything clogging it.

CLEANING AN IRON

The best way to keep most appliances in good working order is to keep them clean, and that applies to your trusty steam iron as well. Unfortunately, if the iron no longer heats or you think it's heating too much, chances are you'll have to take it to a professional, who can get inside the soleplate and either replace the heating element or adjust the thermometer.

You will need	**W H A T T O D O**
white vinegar	1. If the iron is sputtering too much steam when it heats up, the steam holes may be clogged with dirt and mineral build-up.
grill pan from the oven	2. To fix this problem, drain the water out of the iron and fill it with white vinegar.
toothpick	3. Turn the iron on to a hot setting and place it face down on the grill pan from your oven or any other rack that will allow the steam from the iron to run out unimpeded.
fine-grade steel wool	4. Once all the steam has passed through the steam holes, use a toothpick to ream out the holes.
	5. To get rid of burned-on gunk and other marks on the soleplate, make sure the iron is off, then dip fine-grade steel wool in white vinegar and scrub the soleplate until the marks have gone.

D O ' S   A N D   D O N ' T S

[X] Since regular tap water holds varying degrees of minerals, using it inside an iron can hasten mineral build-up around the steam holes and clog them. Use distilled water instead.

3

THE
BIG CLEAN

As difficult as it is to accept, all men know that a woman will not set foot in a filthy house. If she does there's a good chance she won't be back a second time, regardless of whether or not you promise to clean the bathroom. And so the choice has to be made: tidy up a bit or spend your prime years in messy, cluttered solitude.

THE DIRT ON CLEANING PRODUCTS

Good manly housework requires some tough cleaning products and, rest assured, there are hundreds of different types to choose from. Finding the right cleaner depends on what you plan to use it for and this is where you need to know some basic chemistry. Generally, dirt and stains have either a high or a low acid content so it should come as no surprise that cleaners vary in acidity too. The tricky part is getting your head around the fact that, to get rid of a high-acid stain, such as grease, you have to use a low-acid, or alkaline, cleaner such as a degreaser. The chemical reaction between the high and low acids neutralizes the stain so you can wipe it away easily. Just remember: opposites attract. That said, for everyday use, there are such things as all-purpose cleaners, which have a balanced acid content. These will work on all but the toughest stains.

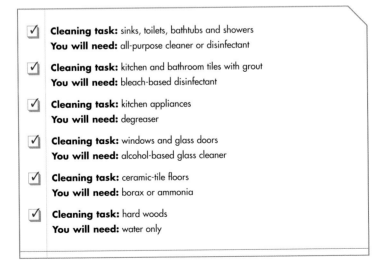

☑ **Cleaning task:** sinks, toilets, bathtubs and showers
You will need: all-purpose cleaner or disinfectant

☑ **Cleaning task:** kitchen and bathroom tiles with grout
You will need: bleach-based disinfectant

☑ **Cleaning task:** kitchen appliances
You will need: degreaser

☑ **Cleaning task:** windows and glass doors
You will need: alcohol-based glass cleaner

☑ **Cleaning task:** ceramic-tile floors
You will need: borax or ammonia

☑ **Cleaning task:** hard woods
You will need: water only

CLEANING TOOLS

While a good broom may not instil the same kind of giddy pride a man gets when he brings home a new table saw, there's no denying that having the right tool makes any job that much easier, even if that job is swabbing out the bathroom.

You will need

long-handled nylon-bristled broom

string mop

sponge mop

vacuum cleaner

bucket

grout brush

scrubbing brush

several sponges with and without scouring pads

terry-towel rags

paper towels

rubber gloves

dustpan and brush

squeegee

duster

WHAT TO DO

1. Designate a separate cupboard for your cleaning gear and install a rack and some hooks inside so you can hang brooms, mops, dusters, dustpans and brushes off the floor.

2. Always keep two buckets on hand – one for soapy water and one for rinsing water. When they're not being used, stack them together and store your rags, rubber gloves and paper towels in one.

HAVING A ROUTINE

To make cleaning more manageable, and therefore more tolerable, it's important to create a routine for yourself. That way, the clutter, the clothes and the dirt won't pile up and you won't have to spend an entire weekend – rather than a few hours each week – digging yourself out.

WHAT TO DO

1. Break cleaning tasks down into four distinct groups: things you can do throughout the day; things you can do at the end of each day; things you can do once a week; and things you can do once a month or even once every few months.

2. The cleaning that you can do throughout the day includes doing the dishes after each meal, wiping down the hob after cooking, putting things away after you've used them and making the bed when you get up.

3. Things to do at the end of each day are picking up the day's clutter, wiping down kitchen worktops, sweeping (if you have wood floors), and gathering stray glasses and dishes to put in the kitchen.

4. Once-a-week cleaning includes dusting, mopping, vacuuming and cleaning the bathroom.

5. Monthly or bimonthly cleaning should include wiping out the oven, scrubbing bathroom tile grout, reorganizing the garage, rearranging the wardrobe and cleaning the windows.

TIP

✓ A good routine to get into during your weekly clean is to include a focus on a different area of the house – your desk in the home office, say – in addition to the normal dusting, sweeping, mopping and bathroom tasks. That way, you'll be tackling the monthly cleaning jobs at the same time you do the weekly ones.

ORDER OF CLEANING

Before you start running around the house willy-nilly and washing everything in sight, step back and make a plan. Otherwise, you risk dirtying what you've just cleaned.

WHAT TO DO

1. Even before you start, you can make the bed you just got out of (see page 46). That's one thing out of the way already.

2. If it's a whole house-cleaning day, the next thing you should do is throw a load of laundry in the washing machine so it can get to work while you're busy.

3. Crank up the stereo and put on your favourite CDs.

4. Pick up any clutter, making sure to get everything that doesn't belong on the floor off the floor.

5. Then break out the duster and give all surfaces, windowsills, picture frames and couch backs a good dusting. Don't worry about pushing dust and debris on to the floor.

6. Sweep and vacuum, making sure you do the bathroom and kitchen floors particularly well. That way, when you finish scrubbing down worktops, sinks, toilets and showers you'll be able to mop up any spilled water straight away.

7. Clean the toilet, then attack the bathtub or shower and the sink. That way, if you rinse off any sponges during the toilet-scrubbing you'll be able to clean up after yourself.

8. Next, clean the kitchen counters, backsplash and appliances.

9. Mop all your hard floors.

10. Put away all the cleaning products and tools.

11. Drink at least one beer.

MAKING THE BED

The experts say that the first step to a clutter-less life is making the bed. If you can do this after waking up every morning (or at least once you've had some coffee), there will always be that one place of calm in the storm.

You will need	W H A T T O D O
one clean fitted sheet	**1** First, place a fitted sheet over the mattress, looping the corners of the sheet over the foot of the bed before doing the head.
one clean top or flat sheet	**2** Spread a top sheet over the mattress so that the sides hang down an equal length and the top edge of the sheet extends all the way up to the head end of the mattress. Let the sheet hang over the foot end of the mattress (see Fig. A).
clean pillowcases	
a duvet, bedspread or some other cover	**3** Tuck the sheet under the foot end of the mattress and at the sides (see Fig. B).
	4 Spread a bedspread over the top sheet, again letting the sides hang down equally on both sides and the foot end of the mattress. Make sure the bedspread is pulled all the way to the top of the mattress at the head end.
	5 Fold the top sheet and the bedspread back on themselves at the head end and to a depth slightly larger than the width of your pillows (see Fig. C).

continued on next page

continued

6 Place the pillows (in clean pillowcases) so that they slightly overlap the end of the sheet and bedspread fold.

7 Now fold the sheet and bedspread back over the pillows, making sure that the bedspread is tucked slightly under the pillows at the front (see Fig. D).

8 Smooth out any wrinkles in the bedspread.

TIP

☑ Making a bed can be done solo, but is always easier with two people. If someone is there to help (especially if that someone shares the bed with you), the job doesn't take more than 5 minutes.

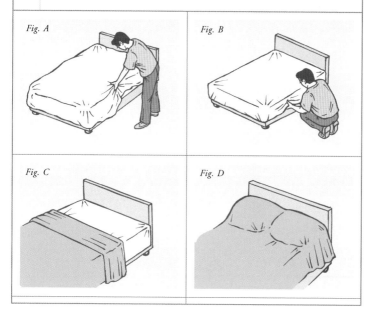

Fig. A

Fig. B

Fig. C

Fig. D

CLEANING A TOILET

This isn't the most glamorous of cleaning jobs, but a man has to do what a man has to do, especially if he plans to invite women into his house. So strap on those rubber gloves, take a deep breath, pick up that sponge and start scrubbing.

You will need	**WHAT TO DO**
rubber gloves	**1** Put on rubber gloves. Spray on or apply the all-purpose cleaner to the inside and outside of the toilet bowl.
bleach-based all-purpose cleaner	**2** Using a sponge, wipe down all surfaces outside the toilet bowl, including the rim, the seat and the seat cover.
sponge	**3** Scrub inside the toilet bowl, making sure you get under the rim of the toilet as well as in the plumbing hole.
toilet-bowl scrubber with nylon bristles	**4** If you have a stubborn ring inside the toilet bowl, turn off the main water supply and flush the toilet. Pour in white vinegar to submerge the ring. Wait a few hours and give the toilet bowl a good, hard scrub. Turn the water back on and flush the toilet.
white vinegar	

SHORT CUT

☑   If you are late for an important meeting at the pub and you didn't get around to cleaning the toilet, pour 50ml (2fl oz) of bleach into the toilet bowl and leave it until you get home. When you return, the toilet bowl should be somewhat clean.

CLEANING SINKS AND BATHS

Bath rings and scum on the sink happen because of a build-up of oil and dirt, and they can get really bad if you live in an area that has "hard" water or water with a high mineral content.

You will need

bucket

non-abrasive all-purpose detergent

nylon-bristled scrubbing brush

dry rag

white vinegar

sponge

bicarbonate of soda

optional:

water softener

WHAT TO DO

1. Fill a bucket with warm water mixed with an all-purpose detergent.

2. Using the nylon-bristled brush, scrub the sink, the bottom and sides of the bath and any fixtures, to remove mineral build-up or bath rings.

3. Rinse everything with fresh water and wipe dry.

4. For particularly stubborn bath rings in fibreglass baths, use undiluted white vinegar on a sponge to remove the marks. Rinse with water.

5. For soap-scum build-up on a sink, sprinkle with bicarbonate of soda and wait 15 minutes before rinsing. Buff to a sparkling shine with a dry rag.

6. If the water where you live has a high concentration of lime or mineral deposits, consider adding a water softener to your water supply.

DO'S AND DON'TS

[X] Don't use a rough scouring powder on a glass-like porcelain bath because it will scratch it and a rough surface will attract dirt and grime much faster than a smooth one.

CLEANING SHOWERS

Ceramic-tile shower and bath walls would be a breeze to clean if there wasn't any grout holding the tiles together and attracting mould. Unfortunately, that's not always the case.

You will need	**WHAT TO DO**
bleach-based tile cleaner	**1** Spray a good amount of bleach-based tile cleaner on to the grout between the tiles and let it sit for 2 minutes.
rubber gloves	**2** Pull on rubber gloves and, using an old toothbrush or grout brush, scrub the grout until it is clean.
old toothbrush or grout brush	**3** Wipe down grout and tiles with a wet sponge.
sponge	**4** Rinse the tiles and grout with water.
	5 To clean shower curtains that have a lot of soap-scum build-up, toss them in the washing machine along with a few towels and add 125ml (4fl oz) of white vinegar or bleach to the mix. Take the curtain out of the machine before the spin cycle and hang it back in the bathroom to dry.

TIP

☑ If you don't have a tile cleaner handy, make your own mould spray by adding 250ml (8fl oz) bleach to 2 pints water.

CLEANING AN OVEN

Though an oven doesn't have to be cleaned every week or even every month (especially for those who never actually use it), the task is still the most unpleasant of all house keeping jobs for two reasons: 1) any spilled food gets baked to a black, carbonated stain that's as hard as concrete; and 2) oven cleaners are as toxic as cleaning products get. Your best defence for an offensive oven is prevention.

HOW TO

1. When food spills, wipe it up immediately (taking care not to burn your hands if the oven is still hot).

2. If you know some food will drip on to the bottom of the oven, get a baking sheet, cover it with aluminium foil and place it under the dish to catch overflow.

3. Wash out the oven with warm soap and water once a week, using steel wool on the tough spots. Don't forget to wipe down the oven door. This keeps you from having to use the toxic oven cleaner and it keeps spilled food from building up and really getting baked on.

4. Buy a self-cleaning oven and skip to the next page.

5. If you do have to use an oven cleaner, spray it on and leave it for about 6 hours before rolling up your sleeves, putting on the rubber gloves and going to work with steel wool or some other heavy-duty scrubbing pad. During this phase, open all windows and doors so that the kitchen is well ventilated. When all the grime and burned-on food has come off, make sure you rinse inside the oven very well.

DOING THE DISHES

Washing the dishes by hand instead of loading them into a dishwasher really isn't that big a deal, especially now that you can buy sponges with handles and built-in soap dispensers.

You will need	**H O W T O**
washing-up liquid	**1** If you're working with a partner, one person can start to wash while the other puts away leftover food and clears the worktops.
soap-dispensing sponge with handle	
regular sponge	**2** If you're by yourself, wrap any leftovers you want to keep and scrape off large crumbs or other gloop left on the plates.
nylon-bristled brush or "scrubbing pad"	**3** Pots, pans or baking trays with cooked-on food should be filled with warm, soapy water and left to soak while you do everything else.
dish drainer	
steel wool	**4** Turn on the water to a low (but not dribbling) pressure and make sure the water is as hot as you can stand it.
bucket (or dog) for food scraps	
	5 To wash an item, use the water from the tap and a soapy sponge to remove any food, using a nylon-bristled brush to get off anything sticky or crusted on.
	6 Rinse the item under the tap and place it in a nearby dish rack to drip-dry.
	7 Do plates and bowls first, then glassware and, finally, cutlery.
	continued on next page

continued

8 Sharp knives, wine glasses or any other special dish should get dried and put away rather than stacked in a rack.

9 After the pots and pans have soaked for a while, use steel wool or a nylon-bristled brush to remove the cooked-on food (it should come off easily after being under water for 10 or 15 minutes). Then use a soapy sponge to wash before rinsing under the tap.

10 When all the dishes are done, wipe down the sink, the worktops and the dining table.

DO'S AND DON'TS

✗ Don't dry the dishes unless you want company or unless you need space. Letting dishes drip-dry is why you have a dish drainer!

✓ Do use rubber gloves, especially if you're doing the dishes with a woman. They think it's sexy to see a man wearing such domestic gear.

DOING WINDOWS

The reason people don't "do windows" isn't because they don't want to spray on a window cleaner and wipe it off. That's the easy part. It's because they don't want to wash both the inside and outside of the window frame and then dust the blinds.

You will need	**H O W T O**
duster	**1** First, dust the windowsills and any moulding that can collect grime.
white vinegar	
rubbing alcohol	**2** Mix up a batch of window cleaner by adding equal parts vinegar and rubbing alcohol to a bucket half-filled with warm water. Funnel some of this mixture into an empty spray bottle.
bucket with warm water	
spray bottle	**3** To clean the inside of a pane of glass, spray on the window cleaner and wipe the window clean. Use a terry-towel rag to buff the window dry.
clean terry-towel rag	
ladder	**4** For the outside-facing glass, carry the bucket with the cleaning mixture outside with you. You may need a ladder to access some windows.
clean, dry rag	
	5 Use a garden hose to wet each window down. Wipe the glass with a rag that has been soaking in the window cleaner, and buff with a dry terry-towel rag.

T I P

☑ It might be helpful to wipe the inside panes back and forth in a horizontal manner and the outside panes in a vertical manner. That way you can easily tell which side has streaks on it.

DUSTING

Dusting, along with sweeping, mopping, doing the dishes and cleaning the bathroom is an essential once-a-week cleaning job.

You will need	**HOW TO**
feather or lamb's-wool duster	**1** Start in the corner of one room and work along the entire wall, dusting everything along the way until you end up back where you started.
mildly damp cloth	
broom handle (optional)	**2** Using a mildly damp cloth or a duster, wipe in a deliberate manner instead of in a sweeping fashion, which can kick up dust instead of collecting it.
	3 Dust the tops of window casings, windowsills, picture frames, cabinets, lampshades and any flat surfaces you come across.
	4 Pillows and couch cushions can be taken outside and beaten with your hand or a broom handle to release the dust.
	5 When your cloth or duster starts to get dirty or filled up with dust, rinse or shake it off and start again.

DO'S AND DON'TS

[X] Don't use furniture polish. It smells like your grandmother's house and can leave a waxy build-up that is worse than dust.

[✓] Pick up picture frames, candles, magazines and other collectibles to wipe underneath them.

SWEEPING

It is said that in life, as in house-cleaning, achieving greatness means we must first master the small and menial tasks. Like most cleaning of a repetitive nature, sweeping can become a meditative, mind-clearing process to be savoured rather than reviled.

You will need	**H O W T O**
sturdy broom with nylon bristles **dustpan and brush** **rubbish bin** **music**	1. As with all cleaning, there should be music playing. Either break up the meditative quality of sweeping by blasting loud rock into the house and street, or put on some sweet harmonies and get into the sweeping groove. 2. Get shoes, chairs and everything else off the floor and on to tables, beds and couches (this chore is made much easier by dealing with the clutter first – see Chapter 1). 3. Unlike mopping, it doesn't matter which room you start in. Simply sweep from the corners and skirtings to a pile in the middle of the floor. Make sure you sweep along the tops of skirtings, too. 4. Sweep the pile into the dustpan and empty into a solid-bottomed rubbish bin.

DO'S AND DON'TS

☑ Do sweep under beds and behind couches and chairs.

☑ Do clean off the dust balls and hair from your broom occasionally.

MOPPING

As with sweeping, you don't have to be super-qualified to mop the floor. Even so, when a floor is mopped it sure can look smart.

You will need	**H O W T O**
string mop	1 If you're dealing with wood floors, use a barely damp string mop, wet only with water, so that you just get rid of the dust.
warm water	
all-purpose cleaner	2 Start in an area furthest from the door so that you don't have to walk on the freshly mopped floor to get to the next room.
two buckets	
more music	3 For tile, vinyl and other hard floors, pour a small amount of all-purpose cleaner into a bucket half-filled with warm water. Also, fill a separate bucket with water for rinsing.
	4 After you get the mop nice and saturated in the solution, wring it out well.
	5 Mop the floor by swinging back and forth in a figure-of-eight motion.
	6 When you see the mop getting dirty, rinse it off in the water-only bucket, wring it out, soak it in the cleaner solution, wring it out again and continue to mop.
	7 When you've finished, rinse the mop once more, wring it out and give the floor a final pass to make sure there isn't any cleaner-solution residue left over.

CHOOSING THE RIGHT VACUUM CLEANER

Picking out the right vacuum for cleaning the house is tantamount to choosing the right lawn mower for your garden. Head on down to your local vacuum store, plug a few of the babies in and give them a test run.

THE STANDARD UPRIGHT

Upright vacuums are the workhorses of the housekeeping world and are perfect for people with plenty of carpet. They work through the combination of a sucking mechanism and an agitator (a spinning brush that "sweeps" as you go). Some come with interchangeable attachments that give you a variety of hoses and nozzles to reach corners.

CANISTER VACUUMS

These smaller types of vacuum are a good choice for those with area rugs and perhaps a carpeted room or two. They work only with a sucking mechanism, through a long hose attached to a cylindrical canister, and are perfect for corners, stairs, edges, even curtains and furniture.

WET-DRY VAC

Wet vacs, as they're commonly known, are heavy-duty vacuums used mostly in woodworking shops or for hosing up flooded basements and overflowing toilets. In addition to being good with water they're great for picking up nails and small bits of wood.

BACKPACK VAC

These cool devices actually strap on to your back, up and out of the way, while you control the nozzle. They're intended for professional commercial cleaners, but who's checking?

VACUUMING A ROOM

Once you've picked out the right machine, take it home and fire it up.

You will need	**H O W T O**
vacuum cleaner	1. First, walk the floor and pick up any loose change, nails, bras and other large objects that could damage the machine.
some flooring	2. Always vacuum away from the cord so you don't have to keep moving it out of the way.
	3. Vacuum in slow, easy strokes instead of fast back-and-forth jabs.
	4. Use an attachment with soft bristles on wood floors so you don't scratch the floor.
	5. Pass twice over areas that have a lot of foot traffic, such as hallways and doorways.

HOW TO CLEAN THE CARPET

Carpet in a man's house is going to get dirty so, if you have it, make sure it's not of the shag variety, which is ten times harder to keep clean than any other. Even then you have to give your rug a deep clean – especially in heavy-traffic areas – once a year. If that doesn't fit into your schedule, at least get dark-coloured carpet to hide the stains, and then call in a professional carpet cleaner to do the dirty work.

You will need	**H O W T O**
vacuum cleaner	1. Start in one room and move all the furniture in that room out of the way.
rented hot-water shampooing machine	2. Go over the carpet at least twice with a vacuum cleaner to get up loose dirt.
hot water	3. Follow the directions on the shampooing machine and fill the appropriate reservoir with hot water and carpet shampoo.
carpet shampoo	4. Push the shampoo machine's vacuum-like hose over the carpet with a slow but steady action. Normally, you will press a button to spray hot water and shampoo into the carpet.
	5. Once you've done an entire room, do it again but, this time, don't press the shampoo button, so that only hot water comes out and rinses the carpet.
	6. The last step is going over the carpet one more time with the machine on a different setting, which allows it to vacuum up much of the water that went into the carpet.

DEALING WITH HOUSEHOLD STAINS

A man's house is bound to get its fair share of stains, what with all the car repair, lawn-mowing and general handiwork going on. That's why it's important to know how to get the stains out.

WOOD

There are times when an absent-minded friend will leave his half-finished cocktail on your favourite wooden coffee table and stain it with a water ring.

You will need	**H O W T O**
white vinegar	1 Mix equal parts vinegar and oil in a small container.
cooking oil	2 Dip a corner of the cloth into the mixture and rub it on to the water ring in the same direction as the grain of the wood until it disappears.
dry cotton cloth	

STONE

Coffee stains on marble or granite worktops can start to look like you're letting things slip a little, even if you just spent the day cleaning out the garage.

You will need	**H O W T O**
flour	1 Make a paste out of flour and hydrogen peroxide and spread a thick amount of it over the coffee stain. Leave it there for 24 hours until dry.
hydrogen peroxide	
putty knife	2 Scrape the paste off with a putty knife and the stain should be gone.

CARPET

If you have carpet or rugs you're going to have stains and that's just the cold hard truth. Here's a list of the most common ones and how to get rid of them.

FOR TEA, COFFEE, SOFT DRINKS, JUICE, MILK, ICE CREAM AND ALCOHOL

You will need	**H O W T O**
1 tsp non-alkaline detergent **8fl oz (250ml) warm water** **rag**	1. Mix the detergent and the water in a container. 2. Soak a clean rag in the solution, wring it out partially, and scrub the stain with the wet cloth. 3. Rinse with warm water.

FOR GREASE, CANDLE WAX AND ANIMAL FAT

You will need	**H O W T O**
1 tsp non-alkaline detergent **1 tsp white vinegar** **8fl oz (250ml) warm water** **two rags** **putty knife** **iron**	1. Mix the detergent, vinegar and water, and work it into the spill with a rag. 2. Do not rinse. 3. Instead, use a dull knife to scrape up the spill. 4. Then put a dry rag over the spill and, with the iron on a warm setting, iron the rag just above the stain. The rag will absorb the spill.

FOR CHOCOLATE, GRAVY AND SHOE POLISH

You will need	**H O W T O**
2fl oz (60ml) detergent **8fl oz (250ml) warm water** **rag**	**1** Mix the detergent and the water in a container. **2** Soak a clean rag in the solution, wring it out partially, and scrub the stain with the wet cloth. **3** Rinse with warm water.

UPHOLSTERY

When your pal isn't leaving cocktail rings on the wooden table, he's slopping cold beer on your new armchair. All is not lost if you act fast.

FOR BEER SPILLS

You will need	**H O W T O**
paper towel **sponge** **50-50 water/white vinegar solution** **water**	**1** First use a paper towel to blot up the froth as soon as it hits the upholstery (waiting to see if your team scores is acceptable, but no longer). **2** Then soak your sponge in the 50-50 water/vinegar solution and work it into and around the stain. **3** Use a paper towel to blot up any excess. **4** Repeat the process with regular water.

4

THE
MATERIAL
FACTS

For a man trying to establish his place in the world, there are three golden rules: get organized, know how to mix a good martini and look good. We've covered the first rule. The second will only come with practice, practice, practice. As for looking good, no one has ever pulled it off wearing dirty, smelly clothes. You have to wash them, and then you have to dry, fold and iron them.

WHY SORT THE WASH?

Much to the disbelief of many men throughout the world, clothes that are going to be washed by machine have to be separated first, by hand, into lights and darks and similar textiles. It's true. Even if you just squandered half your monthly income on the fanciest washing machine out there, this decidedly untechnological chore must be done.

Here's why: dark clothes (especially red ones), when washed with white ones, will bleed and turn your manly white boxer shorts into frothy pink bloomers. It would be tolerable (and perhaps even slightly exciting) if this were to happen to only one pair of boxer shorts, but that's never the case. No, when a rogue piece of dark clothing decides to fade and bleed, it turns every white item in the washing machine the same hazy colour – usually a dull bluish-grey or a murky light pink – just enough so that everyone who sees you (should you choose to wear the offending item) will laugh and point and perhaps even consider you an imbecile for not sorting your clothes.

Also, if you don't sort out linen, polyester, rayon or any other dry-clean-only clothes from the everyday stuff like socks and underwear, there's a fantastic chance that you're going to shrink shirts and trousers into tight, doll-sized garments that only your dog could wear. Bottom line: sort the clothes and keep your wardrobe intact.

THE TEXTILE LABELLING CODE

If you live in a constant state of anxiety that the clothes you wash, dry and iron will come out shrunk, burned, faded or torn, do not fear. A collection of laundry meisters from around the world have created an international textile code used by clothing manufacturers to inform laundry-challenged bods everywhere exactly how to care for their clothes. All you have to do is check the label.

CRACKING THE CODE

	Hand-wash only
	Dry-clean only
	Drying
	Do not tumble-dry
	Do not use chlorine bleach
	Do not iron

WHAT NOT TO WASH

If we could throw the whole house in the washing machine we would, especially the bathroom. Unfortunately, the toilet, bath and sink wouldn't fit. And even though washing machines are for washing clothes, you still can't wash every shirt you own – some have to be hand-washed or dry-cleaned.

WHAT TO DO

1. If you're unsure about any article of clothing, check the label to determine how to care for the material. It could say "dry-clean only" or "hand-wash only". Many will give even more detailed directions, complete with recommended water temperature and drying methods.

2. In general, don't machine-wash any article of clothing made out of fine wool or cashmere, and certainly don't tumble-dry either type of material or it'll shrink to the size of a postage stamp.

3. Don't wash anything that says "dry-clean only", unless the piece of clothing is old, you don't care too much about it and you don't want to pay to get it dry-cleaned. Instead, wash it on a gentle cycle in cold water or hand-wash it and lay it out flat to dry.

4. Don't wash clothes that have spots or stains on them without treating those stains first (see opposite).

5. No matter what you do, never wash any item of clothing that your significant other really likes, especially if you're not willing to look at every single label.

TREATING STAINS

Stains on clothes can signal one of two things: you're a hard worker and you have the grease, dirt and grass stains to prove it; or you're a sloppy eater who doesn't care about his appearance. One will get you a date, the other won't.

You will need	**HOW TO**
stained shirt	**1** If you get spaghetti sauce (or something similar) on clothes, the best thing you can do is act fast.
sparkling water	
cloth	**2** Get the stain thoroughly wet by dabbing it with a cloth soaked in sparkling water. If no sparkling water is available, use plain water and a little hand soap. You should be able to see the stain disappear.
spot remover	
liquid detergent	
	3 If you happen to miss a stain or can't treat it right away, all is not lost. Just dab it with spot remover before putting it in the wash. Lacking that, you can put a bit of liquid detergent directly on to the spot and rub it in.
	4 If the stain doesn't wash out the first time around, let the piece of clothing drip-dry and try the spot remover or detergent again.

DO'S AND DON'TS

[X] Don't use hot water to wash clothes with stains, as this is likely to set the stain for good. Instead wash clothes in cold or warm water.

[X] Don't put stained clothes in a tumble dryer because the heat will only bake the stain in permanently.

WASHING BY HAND

Contrary to what you might be thinking, hand-washing clothes doesn't mean you have to stand knee-deep in a river, beating your trousers against a rock.

You will need	**H O W T O**
bucket **cold water** **Woolite or some other kind of gentle liquid detergent for hand-washing**	**1** Place a bucket in the kitchen sink and fill it up with cold water, adding a capful (at most) of detergent after or just before you turn off the water. **2** With the bucket still in the sink, put the article of clothing in and agitate it with your hand, turning it over and around and generally simulating the gentle cleaning motions of a washing machine. If there's a particularly troublesome spot, rub the area against other parts of the material. **3** Let the clothing sit for 10 minutes in the soapy water before agitating it once more. **4** Remove the clothing from the water and pour the water out of the bucket. **5** Rinse the clothing by filling the bucket up a second time with cold water, this time holding the clothing directly under the stream of water. Make sure you run water over every part of the fabric. **6** Once the bucket is filled, place the clothing in the water and agitate it inside the rinse water to get more soap out. After 5 minutes, if you see a lot of soap inside the bucket or if you can see suds on the clothes, replace the water and rinse again.

continued on next page

continued

7 Do not wring out the clothing, or it will have millions of tiny wrinkles when it dries and you'll risk stretching the material. Instead, hang the clothing up to drip-dry above the bath.

TIP

☑ If you want a hand-washed shirt to dry faster, get a towel of a similar colour and lay it on a flat surface. Put the wet shirt inside the towel and roll the towel up with the shirt inside it. If you push down on the towel, the water from the shirt will seep out and be absorbed. Unroll the towel and the shirt and hang the shirt up to dry further.

WASHING BY MACHINE

You'd be surprised what an entire wardrobe of clean clothes can do for a man's sense of clarity. No more digging around in the laundry basket for that missing sock, no more shoving piles of dirty clothes under the bed and no more sour-smelling towels.

You will need	**HOW TO**
washing machine	**1** Sort clothes into piles of whites, bright colours and darks.
detergent	**2** Remove change, pens, wallets or any paper. Unroll socks, shirtsleeves and trouser legs. Remove underwear from trousers.
owner's manual	**3** Check clothes for spots and stains and treat them with a spot remover or liquid detergent (see page 69).
	4 Put a sorted pile of clothes into the machine, and add the detergent either directly to the drum or to a small drawer on the washing machine's control panel.
	5 Select the type of wash you want. Most times this will be a "normal" or "regular" cycle.
	6 Set the water temperature: warm for whites and cold for bright colours and darks.

TIP

☑ Adding chlorine bleach can help some whites to get whiter but use it sparingly on an article of clothing. Used too much, bleach can disintegrate natural clothing fibres.

DRYING

The greatest fear when dealing with dirty laundry is the dreaded shrinking phenomenon. It can happen in hot water in the washing machine but most often it happens in the silent but deadly tumble dryer. If in doubt, hang clothes up to dry. A little sunlight and fresh air will give them a cleaner smell anyway.

You will need	**H O W T O**
tumble dryer	**1** As you empty the washing machine, set aside any clothes that shouldn't get tumble-dried.
clothesline or drying rack	**2** Hang up these clothes on a clothesline outside or on a drying rack that you can set up in the laundry room.
	3 Set the drying temperature to medium or low. Drying things on hot is really only for towels.
	4 Check the clothes periodically: not all things dry at the same pace (thin cotton sheets will dry much faster than a thick pair of jeans). Taking items out as they dry will extend the life of your clothes significantly.
	5 Fold or hang freshly dried clothes right away to prevent wrinkling.

D O ' S A N D D O N ' T S

Don't dry white clothes with dark ones. Since they're still wet when they first go in the dryer, colours may bleed.

FOLDING

The reason for a good fold is to keep wrinkles at bay. Throw a freshly dried load of clothes on the floor or back in a laundry basket and you'll have more wrinkles than your great-grandma.

HOW TO

1. To fold a T-shirt, lay it face down on a flat surface. Fold one sleeve and one side of the T-shirt to the middle of the back of the shirt and fold the sleeve back on top of the fold. Do the same the other side. Fold the bottom half of the shirt up towards the neck and turn it over.

2. Hang button-down shirts on a coat hanger and make sure the collar is folded down. Fasten the top two buttons to keep the collar straight while it's in the wardrobe. Brush out any wrinkles in the shirt while it's still warm from the dryer.

3. Fold socks in pairs so that they won't get separated: put matching socks together and roll them up starting at the toe. Then tuck the sock ball into the elastic of one of the socks.

IRONING

The best approach to ironing is to get someone else to do it for you. If you have nice shirts, take them to the cleaners and have them professionally laundered and ironed. It costs about £1 a shirt and it's worth it. If you're in a bind and there's no other alternative than to do it yourself, here's how.

You will need	**H O W T O**
new iron filled with distilled water (for steam)	**1** Set the correct iron temperature.
	2 Spread the shirt flat and press the back of the collar first, then the front. Iron from the ends towards the centre, as collars tend to crease.
ironing board	**3** Next iron the cuffs. Open them up and do the insides first and then the outsides.
	4 Iron the sleeves next. Lay them flat on the board and smooth them out so you don't press any creases in the material. Iron in slow deliberate movements. To iron the shoulders, fit the arm-holes over the end of the board.
	5 Iron the body of the shirt last. Lay the shirt so that the collar points towards the narrow end of the board and one front side of the shirt faces you. Iron from the shoulder to the shirttails.
	6 Rotate the shirt. Iron the back next and the other front side last.

T I P

☑ Use a spray bottle filled with water to wet tough wrinkles before running an iron over them.

SEWING AND PATCHING

As the old adage says, a stitch in time saves nine. If you wait, a tear or rip is only going to get bigger. Get yourself a sewing kit to keep around the house. An ideal kit will contain a good selection of different-coloured threads, a variety of different-gauge needles, pins, a pin cushion, a needle threader, extra buttons, scissors and a thimble.

You will need	**W H A T T O D O**
patch	**1** To patch the knee on a pair of jeans, lay the jeans out flat and piece together the torn area as best as possible, smoothing out any wrinkles.
pins	
different-coloured thread	**2** Place your patch over the tear, making sure that it covers the hole completely.
needle	**3** Use pins to secure the patch to the jean leg around the perimeter of the patch. Push the pins through the front of the jean leg only. Also, take care not to move the jeans too much so that the patch remains exactly where you want it.
thimble	
scissors	
	4 Once the patch is thoroughly pinned around the tear or hole, pull off about 60cm (24in) of like-coloured thread from a spool. Thread a needle and pull through to create two 30cm (12in) lengths. This way the thread will be doubled (and therefore stronger).
	5 Tie the loose ends of the thread together and make a knot to keep it from pulling through the fabric.
	continued on next page

continued

6 Put a thimble on the index finger of one hand and put that hand inside the jeans and behind the patch. This hand will be used to hold the jeans and guide the needle while your free hand does all the actual sewing.

7 The first stitch should be started inside the jeans. Make sure it goes through a solid piece of fabric and that the needle comes through the patch about 5mm (¹/₄ in) from its edge. Pull the thread tight.

8 Now, in one motion, put the needle through the top of the jeans just to the side of the patch and bring it back up through the patch about 5mm (¹/₄ in) from where the needle first went in: you are essentially creating tiny loops around the edge of the patch.

9 Repeat the process around all four edges of the patch. When you get back to the first stitch, stop sewing inside the jeans and tie off the thread, using scissors to cut off any excess.

DO-IT-YOURSELF

The house should be pretty clean and organized by now. Even so, a man's work doesn't begin and end with drying and folding a drawer full of underwear. No, sir. Now's the time to get reacquainted with your hammer, electric drill and the other tools of the handyman trade. And remember, DIY projects are a great way to impress girls and build confidence: knowing how to build shelves, replace bathroom tiles and repair plasterboard is tantamount to knowing how to survive in the wilderness with nothing more than some soggy matches and a pocket knife.

THE WORKSHOP

First off, an organized workshop needs space. Most guys make do with a corner of the garage, where there's room for a workbench, some shelves and drawers to store tools in and maybe even a table saw. If you're able to dedicate the whole garage to that purpose, then more power to you. You'll be able to get more tools and have plenty of storage space to keep your stuff.

Either way, there are four things every workshop needs: storage; easy access to tools; ventilation and adequate lighting; and a clutter-free table top or workbench. These are all fairly self-explanatory, but finding enough storage space almost always poses the greatest problems. Before you start to organize your space consider the following storage solutions:

Metal shelves are great for housing large power tools.

Pegboard is essential: it can be attached to the wall above a workbench or it can extend from floor to ceiling. Metal hooks fix into pre-drilled holes and are great for hanging electrical wire, extension cords and tools.

Doorless cabinets with shelves can be installed above a workbench and used for rags, paint tins, spare parts, plumbing pipe and cleaning products.

Small drawers installed under a workbench are ideal for screws, nails, hinges and other hardware.

If you need space for leftover lumber, consider laying it on top of any rafters in the garage or buy two large metal brackets and attach them to the wall high above the floor and out of the way.

Make sure you put similar hand and power tools together: hang saws next to each other on the pegboard; do the same for levels and vices.

Reserve a single drawer for nothing but screwdrivers or nothing but wrenches. If you do this, line the drawer with soft foam so that the tools won't get jumbled around every time you open and close the drawer.

Arrange tools so that the ones you use the most, like screwdrivers, hammers, electric drill and wrenches are easy to get to.

GENERAL TIPS FOR DOING THINGS YOURSELF

Be certain that you can actually do the fix you're attempting and that you can do it in a safe way. It's not great for your image to have to call a professional to come in and finish what you started, nor is it ideal to ask your girlfriend to help you find your missing finger because you've just cut it off with the circular saw.

Don't start a project without having the right tools and materials to finish the job.

Before you start anything, consider what kind of a mess you're going to make and take appropriate precautions. Open windows to let out saw-dust, cover furniture and carpets before painting and put down dust sheets over ceramic tiles or wood floors to prevent scratching them.

Always clean up when you've finished a job.

A MAN AND HIS TOOLS

When new storage is needed or the time comes to fix a wood floor, a man without tools is like a lion without claws. He is helpless. The same could also be said for a man who can't find his tools, even though he owns whatever it takes to get the job done. That's why getting the tools you need and storing them inside an easily accessible and organized workshop is the first step to doing any decent DIY.

Essential tool kit

185mm (7¼ in) circular saw

12-volt drill/screw gun
with drill bits

table saw

router

extension cords

claw hammer with
fibreglass handle

set of Phillips-head and
slothead screwdrivers

steel tape measure

set of chisels

1m (3ft) level

coping saw

crosscut saw

hacksaw

plastic fold-up saw horses

needle-nose pliers

slip-joint pliers

pipe wrench

adjustable wrench

Stanley knife with blades

A Field Guide to Tools, by Steve Dodds

BUILDING DRAWERS

Drawers are a handy way to get organized, and they can be made in a variety of shapes and sizes to store everything from office supplies to pots and pans to bath towels. Whatever the size of the drawer you build, make sure the height and width are 2.5cm (1in) smaller than the opening you want to fill, and the depth is 8cm (3in) shorter.

You will need	**H O W T O**
two 11.5x48x1cm (4³/₄ x 19 x ¹/₂ in) plywood sides	**1** Here are simple drawer plans for a 40cm (16in)-wide by 15cm (6in)-tall by 56cm (22in)-deep opening. The drawer is a simple box with a board stuck on the front to make it look good.
two 11.5x35x1cm (4³/₄ x 14 x ¹/₂ in) pieces plywood for front and back	**2** The measurements for the side panels here account for a 5mm (¹/₄ in) bottom and measurements for the front and back panels account for the two 1cm (¹/₂ in)-thick side panels.
37x48x0.5cm (15x19 x ¹/₄ in) plywood bottom	**3** Fasten the side panels to the front and back panels by hammering lost-head nails every 3.5cm (1 ¹/₂ in), and attach the bottom panel to the box in the same way.
17x42x1cm (7x17x¹/₂ in) plywood face	**4** Centre the face board on the front panel and attach it by screwing the 3cm (1 ¹/₄ in) wood screws through the inside of the front panel and into the face.
hammer	
3¹/₂cm (1 ¹/₂ in) lost-head nails	**5** Attach the drawer handle to the centre of the face board.
screwdriver	
3cm (1¹/₄ in) wood screws	
drawer handle	

BUILDING SHELVES

The more shelves you have, the more space you have to store and organize your stuff. There are the wall-hung bracketed kind, the freestanding metal kind or the complex wooden kind made with dados and mortises. One easy way to build a sturdy set of freestanding wooden shelves is to use cleats – small pieces of wood upon which the shelving boards can rest.

You will need	**H O W T O**
2, 180x2.5x25cm (6x1x10in) boards **12, 22x2.5x2.5cm (9x1x1in) cleats** **6, 100x2.5x25cm (3x1x10in) boards** **sheet of 5mm (¼ in) plywood** **6, 100x2.5x5cm (3x1x2in) "lips"** **tape measure and pencil** **electric drill** **3.5cm (1½ in) flat-head wood screws** **screwdriver** **power saw**	**1** Lay out the two 180cm (6ft) boards on the ground. Starting at what will be the bottom of a bookcase, measure up 2.5cm (1in) and mark that spot with a pencil. From there, measure every 35cm (14in) and make pencil marks at those spots. The bottoms of the shelves will rest at these points. **2** At each pencil mark – and flush with the back of each board – screw in a 2.5x2.5cm (1x1in) cleat, lining up its top with the pencil mark. To make sure the cleat won't split when fastened to the sides, drill three evenly spaced pilot holes into each one, then drive the screw through the cleat face (see Fig. A). **3** Once all the cleats have been attached, hold a 100cm (3ft) "shelf" in place on top of the bottom cleat and drive two screws, equally spaced, through the face of the 180cm (6ft) board into the end of the shelf. Lay the unit on its side and screw the other end of the shelf to the opposite board (see Fig. B). *continued on next page*

continued

4 Leave the unit lying on its side while you secure the top shelf, then the rest of the shelves.

5 Measure and cut the sheet of plywood to fit on the back of the shelving unit. Fasten it with screws, spaced every 25cm (10in) around its perimeter (see Fig.C).

6 To finish the project, attach a "lip" to the front of the unit, under each shelf. Make sure it is flush with the bottom of the shelf and drive one screw into each end through the outer face of the bookshelf sides (see Fig. D).

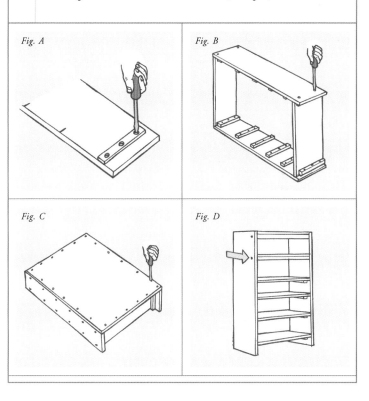

Fig. A

Fig. B

Fig. C

Fig. D

BUILDING CABINETS

A cabinet is essentially just a box with two sides, a top, a bottom (the deck), a back as well as a front (the face frame) and a door. It can be used to store anything from glassware to CDs to television sets, as long as you add in a few shelves or drawers. Building a cabinet like the one below is fairly easy although you're going to need some good power tools – at last, I hear you say!

You will need	**H O W T O**
2.5cm (1in) plywood	1 Measure out two 60x75cm (24x30in) pieces of 2.5cm (1in) plywood for the two side panels of the cabinet and cut them out using a circular saw.
2cm ($^3/_4$ in) plywood	2 On each one measure up 2.5cm (1in) from the bottom and draw a line at that mark. This is where you'll cut the dado, a 2cm ($^3/_4$ in)-wide by 8mm ($^3/_8$ in)-deep groove on the inside of the cabinet that the deck will fit into snugly.
circular saw	
tape measure	
carpenter's pencil	
table saw with 2cm ($^3/_4$ in) dado blade	3 Cut a dado along the pencil lines, using a table saw with a dado blade.
electric drill	4 Next cut rabbets along the back and top edges of each side panel. Rabbets are just like dados except they are cut into the end of a board to act as a 8mm ($^3/_8$ in)-deep ledge support for an attaching board. In this case they will support the 2cm ($^3/_4$ in)-plywood back and top of the cabinet.
hammer	
6cm (2$^1/_2$ in) lost-head nails	

continued on next page

continued

5 Measure out a piece of 2cm ($^3/_4$ in) plywood for the deck, taking into consideration the 2cm ($^3/_4$ in) width of the rabbet on the back of the sides (you don't want the deck to extend past the rabbeted edge) and the 8mm ($^3/_8$ in)-deep dado. Cut it out using a circular saw.

6 Slide the deck into the dados on the two sides so that its front edge is flush with the sides' edges. Secure it in place by nailing through the face of the side panels, through the dado and into the end of the deck every 10cm (4in).

7 Now you can measure for the top of the cabinet, which will be as deep as the sides are wide and as long as the distance between the inside ends of the two sides plus a total of 2cm ($^3/_4$ in) (for the two 8mm ($^3/_8$ in)-deep rabbets). Once you get your measurements correct, cut out the cabinet top.

8 Cut a rabbet in the back underside edge of the top panel (to support the back) and lay it in place so that its ends are sitting on the rabbet ledges. Fasten the top to the sides with 6cm ($2^1/_2$ in) lost-head nails spaced every 10cm (4in).

9 Measure and cut out the cabinet back and nail it on.

10 Finish the front of the cabinet by nailing 2.5x5cm (1x2in) pieces of 2cm ($^3/_4$ in) plywood over the ends of the sides, the top and the deck.

T I P

✓ Measure twice, cut once.

✓ If you're making a cabinet for the kitchen, bathroom or anywhere that will expose the structure to water, use regular "marine" plywood rather than chipboard, which can expand and weaken when wet.

REPAIRING A HOLE IN PLASTERBOARD

Most cleaning and taking care of minor repairs happens when you're getting ready to throw a cocktail party. There are occasions, however, when you find yourself doing the repairs once everyone leaves. One such instance is patching a hole or two in plasterboard: after all, you never know when a guest may punch, kick or fall headfirst into your living-room wall.

You will need	**HOW TO**
keyhole saw	1 If the hole is roundish in shape (the size of a fist, shoe or head, for example), use a keyhole saw and turn the round hole into a square one.
Stanley knife	
scraps of plasterboard	2 Make sure there is no loose plaster or paper around the perimeter of the hole. If there is, break or cut them off, using a Stanley knife.
drill	
plasterboard adhesive	3 Cut a scrap of plasterboard to the same size as the hole plus about 5cm (2in) all around. This is the backer board.
putty knife and Polyfilla	4 Drill a finger-sized hole in the middle of the backer board.
plasterboard tape	5 Run a bead of plasterboard adhesive on the backer board, around the outer edges of its face so that it will stick to the wall behind the hole.
fine-grit sandpaper	
	6 Put the backer board inside the hole and, using your finger and the finger hole, hold it in place for several minutes until the adhesive takes hold.
	continued on next page

continued

7 Now cut a piece of plasterboard to the same size as the hole. This is the patch.

8 Smear plasterboard adhesive on the back of the patch.

9 Fit the patch into the hole with its back resting against the backer board and hold it there briefly until the adhesive dries.

10 Spread a light layer of Polyfilla along the edges of the patch using a putty knife, then push plasterboard tape into the Polyfilla.

11 Cover the tape with another layer of Polyfilla and smooth more Polyfilla over the entire patch, making sure you blend the edges into the surrounding plaster. Let it dry.

12 After the Polyfilla has dried, sand it smooth all over, using fine-grit sandpaper.

13 Paint the wall to hide the patch altogether.

H I N T

Instead of holding the backer board in place you can tie one end of a piece of twine to a pencil, put the pencil through the finger hole and tie the other end of wire to a long piece of wood, which acts as a brace.

REPLACING A MANTEL

If you have a fireplace chances are it's the centre of attention for everyone who walks in. That means if you're grilling steaks or cooking large pots of beans on the hearth you might want to move the operation outside to the barbecue. Then you might want to make things a bit more cosy and inviting. Put a whisky bottle nearby and lay down a soft yak-wool carpet. Then scrub the bricks or stone to get the soot off, and if the mantel is rotting or run down either paint it or replace the surround altogether. Antique or salvaged mantelpieces can bring a lot of style to a young man's pad and they're not hard to install.

You will need	**H O W T O**
new or antique fire surround	1 First, remove the old mantelpiece by prying it away from the wall with a crowbar or claw hammer. Make sure you put a block of wood between the tool and the wall so you don't gouge or break the plasterboard.
crowbar or claw hammer	
wood blocks	2 Once the old mantel is gone, locate the studs in the wall around the fireplace opening and mark their location.
pencil	
spirit level	3 Centre the mantel around the fireplace opening.
wood shims	4 Level it by placing a spirit level on the top shelf. Use wood shims under one side or the other to ensure a proper level (see Fig. A).
electric drill and drill bits	
9cm (3¹/₂ in) lost-head nails	

continued on next page

continued

hammer

nail punch

wood filler

sealant and sealant gun

paint (optional)

5 Using an electric drill and drill bits just smaller than the nails you plan to use, drill pilot holes through the mantel and into the wall every 25 cm (10in) along the sides and top.

6 Drive 9cm (3¹/₂ in) lost-head nails into the pilot holes to fix the mantel to the studs in the wall (see Fig. B).

7 Use a nail punch to drive the nail heads below the surface of the wood and fill the holes with wood filler coloured to match the mantel.

8 Seal any gaps between the mantel and the wall and paint it if you want to. Just don't paint it if it's mahogany, oak or some kind of South American hardwood. Trust me on this one.

Fig. A

Fig. B

HOW TO REPLACE A CRACKED CERAMIC TILE

Cracked or loose bathroom tiles can really compromise your bathroom-cleaning efforts. It looks bad and the cracks will gather mould and mildew faster than you can clean them.

You will need	**H O W T O**
scoring knife with carbide-tipped blade	**1** Using a carbide-tipped scoring knife, rake out the grout around the broken tile.
hammer	**2** Use a hammer and chisel to break out the tile and remove the pieces from the wall. Also remove any old dried adhesive behind the tile so that the wall surface is totally flat.
chisel	
putty knife	**3** Smear a good amount of mortar on the back of the new tile and press it into place until it is flush with the surrounding wall.
mortar	
rubber gloves	**4** Put on rubber gloves and press grout cement into the gaps around the new tile.
grout cement	
wet rag	**5** After 15 minutes, wipe off excess grout with a wet rag. If there are gaps or holes in the grout, apply more, let it set for 15 minutes, and wipe the excess off again.

D O ' S   A N D   D O N ' T S

[X] Don't let grout cement or mortar dry on the face of any tile.

[✓] Remove dried grout cement or mortar with paint thinner.

GETTING A SQUEAK OUT OF A WOOD FLOOR

Squeaks in wood floors result from either the wood or the subfloor warping and leaving a gap between the two. When you step on the floor above such a gap, the wood rubs on a nail or against another board and makes a squeak. This can be a real nuisance, especially if you're trying to sneak into the house after a long night drinking with the guys.

You will need	**HOW TO**
electric drill with 2.5mm (^{3}/32 in) drill bit	1. Locate the squeaky part of the floor and drill two small holes through the face of the wood. Make sure the holes are 5cm (2in) apart and that they are drilled at an angle towards each other and into the subfloor below.
hammer	
6cm (2^1/2 in) lost-head nails	2. Hammer a 6cm (2^1/2 in) lost-head nail through each hole and into the subfloor.
nail punch	3. Use a nail punch to drive the nail below the surface of the finished wood floor.
wood filler	4. Fill the nail holes with wood filler.
	5. Repeat this process anywhere you find a squeak.

DO'S AND DON'TS

[X] Don't hammer the nail so far that you hit the wood itself.

[✓] Use a coloured wood filler to match the colour of the wood stain on the floor.

PATCHING A HOLE IN A WOOD FLOOR

Dragging metal furniture around on a tongue-and-groove hardwood floor is not a good idea. Dropping a bowling ball on one is worse. But these things do happen.

You will need	**H O W T O**
varying lengths of matching tongue-and-groove wood in the same width	**1** Figure on replacing the entire length of the damaged boards. This way, the seams of the new boards will not line up, and the patch will blend in to the surrounding floor better.
masking tape	**2** Tape off the boards to the right and left of the damaged boards so that you don't end up replacing any undamaged boards by mistake.
circular saw	
crowbar	
hammer	**3** Set your circular saw to cut to the depth of the thickness of the flooring, usually about 2.5cm (1in). Cut along the length of each board that needs replacing (see Fig. A).
6cm (2½ in) lost-head nails	
table saw	**4** Push a crowbar into the cuts and pry out the cut boards to reveal the plywood subfloor underneath.
	5 Cut lengths of new wood to fit into the spaces left by the damaged boards. Fit the groove of the first board over the tongue of the first undamaged board and hold it tightly in place (see Fig. B).
	continued on next page

continued

6 Hammer a 6cm (2½ in) lost-head nail through the face of the board and into the subfloor every 15–20cm (6–8in). For the last board, it may be necessary to cut off the bottom lip of its groove so that it can fit snugly in place (see Fig. C).

7 Once the new wood has been set, sand the entire floor and stain it all the same colour (see Fig. D).

DO'S AND DON'TS

☑ Take special care where cut and damaged boards line up next to boards that don't need replacing, as it is easy to break wooden tongues.

Fig. A

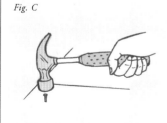

Fig. B

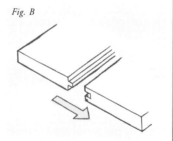

Fig. C

Fig. D

REWIRING A LAMP

One of the best ways to improve the atmosphere of a dim, dark space is to add more light, but don't just settle for overhead fittings. Get yourself some cool, retro, flea-market lamps for the living room and clean them up a bit: first buy new lampshades. Then check the wiring and the plug. If either is rusty or frayed the electricity could short out and start a fire, which would not be good (it certainly wouldn't do anything to improve the look of your house).

You will need	**H O W T O**
screwdriver	**1** Remove the lampshade and the "gimbal" that holds the shade in place (see Fig. A).
wire cutters	
new flex	**2** Unscrew the socket from the lamp base and pull it, with the cord still attached, away from the base. Pull the outer shell and the cardboard or plastic sleeve off the socket to expose the screw terminals that the flex is attached to.
wire stripper or pocket knife	
new plug	**3** Cut the old flex and pull it out of the lamp base completely, but don't take off the flex from the screw terminals on the socket. Thread a new flex into the lamp and out of the top (see Fig. B).
	4 You're going to attach the new flex to the socket in the same way the old flex was attached. Unscrew the screw terminals to remove the old flex. With your wire stripper or pocket knife remove the surrounding plastic from the new flex (see Fig. C). Connect the new flex to the two screw terminals.

continued on next page

continued

5 Reassemble the outer shell, sleeve and socket to the lamp. Replace the gimbal and shade.

6 Add a new plug by stripping the other end of the flex and threading it into the plug. Attach the new flex to the plug's screw terminals and voila! Instant atmosphere (see Fig. D).

DO'S AND DON'TS

✗ Never stand in water when dealing with electricity.

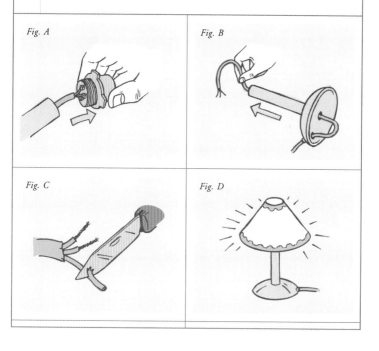

Fig. A

Fig. B

Fig. C

Fig. D

INTERIOR MAINTENANCE

So now you can do a few things to fix up the house a bit. But if there's a leaky plumbing pipe, a squirrel in the insulation or dry rot in the floorboards, it won't matter how often you clean the toilet or build bookshelves, your pad will go to seed faster than you can say "home maintenance". Just don't forget that on the big dangerous jobs, it's sometimes better to hire a professional to fix the problem rather than to try doing it yourself. Not only do you still get all the credit for keeping the house in order but you get to stay out of hospital as well.

PLUMBING: BURST PIPES

Freezing temperatures are not what your plumbing pipes look forward to. This is when they crack or burst because the water inside them expands as it freezes. If a pipe does burst, there's no time to waste. First stop the leak with a temporary patch – there are several ways to do this – then call a plumber.

You will need	**WHAT TO DO**
duct tape	**1** If the crack looks small and the leak is gradual, it may be possible to wrap the pipe with duct tape without turning off the main water supply. Make sure you overlap each pass of tape as you cover the crack.
epoxy glue or paste	
pipe clamp	
hose clamp	**2** A more permanent patch can be made with shop-bought epoxy glue or paste, especially if the crack is near a pipe joint. Before applying any epoxy, the water must be turned off and the pipe must be thoroughly dry.
rubber pad	
screwdriver	
	3 For a larger crack, turn the water off once you have located the leak, then place a rubber pad over the crack and around the pipe. Put half a "C"-shaped pipe clamp over the rubber, on top of the pipe. Fit the other half of the clamp in place so that it surrounds the rubber and the pipe, and screw the two halves together. (If you don't have a pipe clamp, a hose clamp (or two or three) will also work.)

continued on next page

continued

4 If you've turned the water off to patch the leak, turn it back on and observe the patched section of pipe to make sure it's not leaking any more.

H I N T

✓ Prevent burst pipes in the first place by installing a stop-and-waste valve on water lines. These allow you to drain water out of pipes in anticipation of freezing temperatures. Also, you can insulate outdoor or basement pipes with foam-plastic pipe insulation or some other commercial wrapping.

HEATING AND INSULATION

As you get your house in order, and as the colder months approach, you'll want to start thinking about insulation. The attic is the most crucial place to have both the right kind and the correct amount of insulation. The next most important place is the floor, especially if you live in a house that has a crawl space underneath. Normally, local building codes recommend how much insulation should be in each of these spaces.

There are many types of insulation out there, but batt insulation and loose-fill insulation are the two types you're most likely to run into in your attic or at the hardware store.

BATT INSULATION

The most common kind is fibreglass, which comes in giant rolls. To install any kind of batting, all you have to do is cut sections of it off the roll with a Stanley knife and push them into wall, floor or ceiling cavities. When dealing with fibreglass, make sure you wear a dust mask and long sleeves because fibreglass slivers are microscopic and can damage lungs and irritate the skin.

LOOSE-FILL INSULATION

Loose-fill insulation is sprayed or blown into attics and walls, using a machine. Its main advantage over batting is its ease of installation and the fact that you're not left with any seams through which cold air can seep into the living space. Fibreglass and wool are used as loose-fill materials but cellulose, which is basically recycled newsprint, is gaining popularity because of its environmental qualities.

WHAT TO DO

1 Climb up into the attic and check for evidence of rodents or other nesting animals. They can chew away insulation and affect its efficiency. If you see evidence, replace the insulation and get rid of the rodents.

2 Check to see that batting or loose-fill insulation is covering every part of the attic. Fill any areas that are not covered with new insulation.

3 Make sure the doorway to the attic is properly insulated. If it's a pull-down panel in the hall ceiling, cut a piece of plywood to fit over it and staple batting to the top of the plywood.

4 If you live in a house with a crawl space, get under the house and check for insulation. If it's an older house, chances are there won't be any, in which case, you can buy batting at the hardware store along with a staple gun and fit it between the floor joists yourself.

5 Walls are difficult to insulate in an old house where the plasterboard is already up. One good solution is to hire a professional who will bore doorknob-sized holes every 40cm (16in), put in a hose and blow in cellulose or other loose fill. They will usually plug the holes with foam or wood plugs, and then finish off the job with Polyfilla and a putty knife. A good paint job is usually required afterwards.

HOT WATER HEATERS

Water heaters seem to work for ever without any problems until the depth of winter when you desperately need a steaming hot bath. Alas, like all appliances, they need some maintenance, especially if the tank is over 10 years old. If that's the case, it might be time to start thinking about getting a new one or at least finding out what to do if something goes wrong.

WHAT TO DO

1. If the water won't stay hot for more than one shower (and there are two people in the house), consider increasing the thermostat setting, which may be a red knob at the base of the water tank. If that doesn't work, you may need to get yourself a larger tank.

2. If the water is too hot, turn the thermostat down. If it doesn't seem to work at all, call a pro.

3. If there is no hot water at all, the pilot light may have gone out or the heater may have blown a fuse. For the latter, check the fuse box and turn the circuit back on. To re-ignite a pilot light, check the instructions that should be posted on the tank itself. Usually, the procedure involves turning the thermostat to "pilot", holding a match over the pilot hole, and pressing a reset button for about a minute.

4. If you smell gas, turn off the main gas supply immediately and call a pro.

HINT

☑ To save as much as 10% on electricity or gas bills, wrap your tank in an insulated "jacket" so that the burner doesn't have to work as hard to keep the water hot.

BOILER CARE

Boilers, like any other appliances or machines, can break down unless they're properly cared for. In this case, though, "breaking down" can mean trouble, especially if it's the middle of winter and there's gas leaking all over the place. To keep a boiler running smoothly, and for a long time, give it a checkup every autumn, and for this particular job, don't hesitate to call in a pro.

You will need		**W H A T T O D O**
long-handled wire brush	1	Before getting started, switch off the main fuel line to the boiler as well as the main electricity.
dust mask	2	Locate the heating chamber on the boiler and, using a long-handled wire brush, swish out the inside to get rid of soot, dirt or any other build-up. Wear a dust mask for this job, and use a heavy-duty wet vac to vacuum up the debris.
heavy-duty wet vac		
duct tape		
	3	Replace the air filter, which you should find inside its own slot right where the metal duct comes out of the unit.
	4	Check the blower fan to make sure there aren't any obstructions and the fan belt to make sure it's tight enough.
	5	Inspect exhaust ducts, especially around joints, and wrap any loose connections with duct tape.

WOODWORM AND TERMITE INFESTATION

Woodworm, termites, and other wood enemies, such as dry rot and wet rot, can do serious damage to a house. That's why finding these trouble spots before they get serious can make the difference between having to do a quick fix and having to undertake major renovation. The most destructive woodworm is the furniture beetle, a brown-black creature that eats wood to survive. These beetles fly into a house and lay their eggs; the grubs hatch and tunnel into structural timbers as well as furniture.

You will need	**WHAT TO DO**
flashlight	**1** To check for wood rot, walk around the perimeter of your house, looking for any wood that is touching the ground. Look especially closely in crawl spaces, on windowsills, wooden stairs and in areas that are perpetually damp.
screwdriver	
old clothes you don't mind getting dirty	**2** A tell-tale sign of any invasion is the presence of woodworm holes and deposits of fine dust, or in the case of termites, the brown mud tunnels they use to get from their colonies in the ground to new sources of food.
	3 To check for wet rot, look for cracks, peeling paint or splits in wood as well as fungus growing on wood, especially in damp areas near plumbing.

continued on next page

continued

4 To check for dry rot, look for cracks and white, dust-like strands or patches on wood.

5 Push the tip of a screwdriver into any suspect wood with your hand. If the tool breaks through the wood and sinks in about 1cm (^{1}/2 in), then you're likely to have woodworm, termites or dry rot.

6 Getting rid of infestation takes a tough approach. The traditional, and most effective, practice – one that pest experts have been using for decades – is to saturate the affected wood with insecticides.

HINTS

☑ Keeping foundations dry goes a long way to controlling wood rot: to keep rainwater from gathering next to foundations, slope the earth away from the house; look for and contain any leaks in basement or crawl-space plumbing pipes.

☑ Control humidity levels in crawl spaces and attics by adding more ventilation: ridge vents are great for keeping fresh air circulating in attics; vent grills should be located every metre (yard) in foundation crawl spaces.

GOOD INDOOR AIR QUALITY

Having good indoor air quality doesn't mean loading up your pad with sweet-smelling candles and incense to get rid of musty odours. On the contrary, it means getting rid of the candles and incense (and the smoke that comes with them) along with any other air-borne allergens such as cigarette smoke, pet fur, pollen spores and common dust mites, which can turn a normal person into an itchy-eyed, stuffy-nosed, scratchy-throated wreck.

HOW TO

1. The least costly and most effective way to improve your indoor air quality (IAQ) is to keep your house clean and free of dust. Dusting, vacuuming, sweeping and mopping on a regular basis are all essential.

2. If you're still tearing up and sneezing from day to day, then you might have to take more drastic measures. Leave windows closed when there's a high pollen count outdoors. If you smoke, either quit or start smoking outside. Indoor pets should be taken outside or at least kept out of the bedroom.

3. If those last two are easier said than done, it is possible to buy air cleaners that actually trap air-borne particles with some kind of filter.

4. The cheapest kind of filters are a disposable pleated type, known commonly as mechanical filters. These are usually made out of fibreglass housed inside a cardboard frame and they need to be changed once every two months or so. Vacuum cleaners also use these filters to keep the dust down.

5. Portable air cleaners that look like small, round or square, high-tech, upended rubbish bins can be bought with a range of filtration devices, depending on your needs.

continued on next page

continued

6 Electrostatic filters actually use an electronic field to attract particles, which stick to a series of flat plates inside the cleaner.

7 Another type of portable filter is called an ion generator. They charge airborne particles so that they are attracted to walls, curtains, furniture or anything else that has a flat surface. The problem with these, though, is that when you sit on the furniture or rustle the curtains the particles take to the air once again.

CLEANING A CHIMNEY

There may be self-cleaning ovens, but for a chimney a man gets no such luck. These smokestacks can collect lots of soot from burning wood as well as all kinds of detritus falling in from above, including birds, branches and other outdoor surprises.

You will need	**H O W T O**
newspaper	1. Lay old newspaper down inside the fireplace to catch any soot or ash as it falls, and hang a sheet around the fireplace opening to keep dust to a minimum. It may also be a good idea to move any furniture away from the area.
old sheet	
steel chimney-sweeping brush	
rope	2. Close the chimney flue.
lead weights	3. Attach a steel chimney-sweeping brush to the end of a long rope, and tie lead weights around the neck of the brush to give it more sweeping power once it's inside the chimney.
soot-coloured clothing	
dust mask	4. Put on soot-coloured clothes, dust mask and goggles and climb a ladder to the top of the roof, taking the brush, weights and rope.
goggles	
ladder	
heavy-duty vacuum cleaner	5. Lower the brush into the chimney and pull it back up repeated times until it stops bringing up soot, ash, twigs or anything else that might be building up inside.

continued on next page

continued

6   Go back inside the house and carefully reach behind the sheet and open the chimney flue to let any soot fall on to the old newspaper.

7   Once the dust has settled, remove the sheet and newspapers. Put the paper in the bin and take the sheet outside to shake out before putting it in the washing machine.

8   Use a heavy-duty vacuum cleaner to get up any debris inside the fireplace.

DO'S AND DON'TS

✗   Don't climb a ladder unless you're sure it's set on firm solid ground. Better yet, get someone to hold it steady while you do the dirty work.

EXTERIOR MAINTENANCE

First impressions can often make the difference between a good first date and a disastrous one. And just as you want to be well groomed for that first date, you want your house to look good when visitors come over. The inside should be organized, clean and in good repair, but it's the outside that gives people that crucial, initial impact. If the paint is flaking or the gutters are falling down, it won't matter how shiny and Zen-like you've made the rest of the house.

GENERAL TIPS FOR DOING EXTERIOR MAINTENANCE

When it comes down to it, your house's main enemy is not your rowdy, football-watching, beer-drinking pals; it's the weather. Rain, wind, sun and snow beat down on roofs, paintwork and windows with so much unrelenting consistency that, sooner or later, you are going to lose a roof tile, find a broken window pane or spot some cracked paint. Even the smallest thing can become a major problem if it is not fixed immediately.

WHAT TO DO

1. Come up with a schedule of repairs that should be done by a certain time of year. Clean out gutters before autumn leaves start to fall and again once they have fallen. Check the roof and make repairs before winter rains come. If you need to paint the house do it in the summer, after the rainy season.

2. Working on the outside of a house usually means being up a ladder. Always make sure the feet of the ladder are resting on flat, solid ground. Don't reach too far off to one side or the ladder might fall. A good rule of thumb is always to keep your hips aligned with the sides of the ladder.

3. Pick up and put away tools after you've worked outside. There is no better way to lose a screwdriver than to leave it lying in the grass overnight.

4. Never underestimate the intrusive power of water. It can get into the smallest nail hole or the faintest hairline crack. Once it gets under roof tiles and into the house, the damage can be costly and a real pain to fix. It's always best to stop water leaks before they get to that point.

5. As with major interior problems, if the job is going to be too time-consuming or too complex, the manly thing to do is to get someone to do the job right: in other words, don't be afraid to hire a pro.

REPLACING A SCREEN

Just like the rest of your house exterior, window screens can start to look worn and shabby as they get older. Not only is it important to keep them clean with a bristle brush and some water, but when holes, tears and general wear give your screens that run-down look, they should be replaced altogether.

You will need	**H O W T O**
fine mesh screen (it should measure a little wider and 15cm (6in) longer than the screen opening)	**1** Remove the old screen from the wooden frame.
	2 Lay the new screen in position, making sure it fits on both sides and at the bottom. (It should overlap the wood frame by 15cm (6in) at the top.) Staple the bottom edge to the wood frame.
stiff putty knife	**3** Using upholstery pliers, grab the middle of the screen at the top and use the wood frame as a fulcrum to pull the screen tight. Staple the top edge of the screen to the wood frame, starting in the middle.
staple gun	
pair of upholstery-stretcher pliers	
hammer	**4** Work your way out to one corner, pulling the screen with the pliers and stapling every 1cm (1/2 in) and then work your way to the opposite corner in the same manner.
panel pins, or tacks	
Stanley knife	**5** Staple the screen to both sides of the wood frame.
	6 Cut off the excess screen with a Stanley knife, and use a hammer and panel pins, or tacks, to fix the moulding back in place.

DRAUGHT-PROOFING A DOOR

If you're eager to show off some new handyman skills but don't want to dive in too deep, draught-proofing a door is the job for you. Simply by adding strips of foam around the door jamb you'll be keeping cold air outside where it belongs instead of inside where it will balloon your heating bills.

You will need	**H O W T O**
measuring tape	**1** Measure the sides and top of the door stop – the strip of wood on the door jamb against which the door closes (see Fig. A).
self-adhesive foam stripping	
scissors	**2** Cut foam stripping to those measurements.
draught excluder	**3** Peel off the backing on the stripping and press it into place on the door stop. When the door closes it will now come up against these foam strips, thereby creating a tighter seal against outside air (see Fig. B).
snips	
screwdriver	
	4 Next, measure the bottom of the door. Cut a strip of foam to fit and stick it to the bottom of the door to provide a seal against the threshold (see Fig. C).
	5 For a tighter seal at the threshold, install a metal draught excluder on the inside of the door.
	6 First cut the draught excluder to fit the door, using tin snips. Then screw it to the face of the door so that the rubber "sweep" comes to rest firmly against the threshold when the door is closed (see Fig. D).
	continued on next page

DO'S AND DON'TS

☑ Leave about 1mm (1/16 in) from the side of the door to the end of the door sweep.

Fig. A

Fig. B

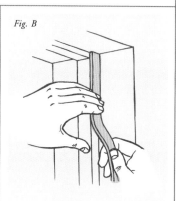

Fig. C

Fig. D

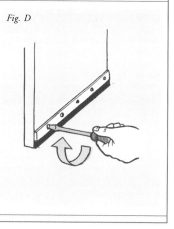

REPLACING AN ASPHALT ROOF TILE

If your roof is covered in asphalt tiles, and many are these days, there's always a chance that one or two will get torn by falling branches or be blown off in a storm. Luckily, replacing an asphalt tile is an easy fix, as long as you don't put off the repair too long. Without roof tiles, there's nothing except plywood and a little roofing felt keeping rain out of your attic.

You will need	**HOW TO**
a new tile the same size and colour as the ones already on your roof	1. Have the intact tile ready, just above the one you're going to replace.
small crowbar	2. Use a small crowbar to remove any nails holding the damaged tile to the roof, and remove any part of the old tile that may be left on the roof.
Stanley knife	
hammer	3. Slide the replacement tile into place. If it doesn't go in easily, cut off the upper corners with a Stanley knife.
3cm (1¼-in) roofing nails	4. Hammer in nails to secure the new tile to the roof battens.
waterproof cement	5. Use waterproof cement to cover the nail heads so that water can't seep in.

TIP

☑ The best time to repair an asphalt roof is on a warm day when the tiles are more pliable. Cold weather stiffens asphalt tiles, which means they're more likely to crack when you're handling them.

REPAIRING ROOF FLASHING

While you're up on the roof replacing a tile, go ahead and check the flashing – the strips of metal found around chimneys and vent pipes and along roof valleys and eaves. These strips are fastened with nails and waterproof cement in places where water has the best chance of leaking into a house. They can get old and come loose or simply start to corrode.

You will need		**WHAT TO DO**
hammer	1	Check flashing at any seams and near its edges. Look for nails that have wiggled loose, crumbling or missing roof cement or any spots that have been bent away from the roof surface.
waterproof cement		
silicone sealant		
strips of aluminium roof flashing	2	Rehammer loose nails, then cover the nail heads with waterproof cement.
wire brush	3	If you see crumbling roof cement or if the metal is bent away from the roof, add more cement or silicone sealant to fill the gap and bend the metal back into place if possible.
putty knife		
	4	If flashing is corroded or has started to form holes, you can patch sections with strips of similar metal.
	5	First, scuff the surface of the old flashing with a wire brush.
	6	Use a putty knife to apply a coat of waterproof cement to the scuffed surface of the old flashing and push the metal patch into the cement and over the corrosion or hole.
	7	Cover the patch with waterproof cement.

SERVICING GUTTERS

As long as the gutters are doing their job – funnelling rainwater off the roof and into a downpipe – we don't think much about them. It's only when they clog up or spring a leak that we start cursing our luck. To avoid this happening to you, start giving your gutters a clean and a checkup twice a year to make sure they keep doing their job.

You will need	**W H A T T O D O**
garden gloves	1 Leaves, twigs, acorns, dead insects and other detritus will fill and clog gutters by the end of autumn, so giving them a good clean both before and after the season is a good idea. (If you live under a bunch of trees that shower their leaves more than most, you might want to check the gutters a few times during autumn as well.)
ladder	
bucket or bin bag	
garden hose	
drainage rod	
screwdriver	2 Put on some gardening gloves and climb a ladder to access the gutters.
silicone sealant	
scrap of aluminium flashing	3 Scoop out leaves and other stuff with your hands and put the rubbish into a bucket or bin bag.
waterproof cement	4 Once you've cleared away the debris, use a garden hose to run fresh water along the gutter (and out the downpipe) as a cleanser.
putty knife	
wire brush	5 If the downpipe is clogged, use a spray attachment on the end of the hose to send a jet of water down the opening. If that doesn't work, use a drainage rod to push the clog out.

continued on next page

continued

6   After the gutters have been cleaned, walk around the perimeter of your house and check for loose screws where sections of gutter meet each other, especially at downpipes. Also, check for loose gutter brackets – the metal straps and spikes that attach the gutters to the roof eave. Tighten either as you go and fill gaps in the metal with silicone sealant.

7   If the gutter has a hole in it (either from rust or a stray tree branch), patch it on the inside of the gutter using a scrap of aluminium flashing and waterproof cement.

8   When the inside of the gutter is perfectly dry, use a wire brush to scuff up the area around the tear or hole inside the gutter, and use a putty knife and apply waterproof cement to the area around the hole.

9   Bend a piece of aluminium flashing to fit the round contour of the gutter and push it into the waterproof cement so that it is securely seated.

10 Apply more waterproof cement around the edges of the patch.

DO'S AND DON'TS

☒ If any part of the gutter is rusted, torn and full of holes, don't try to patch it. Just replace the entire section.

☒ When patching a hole inside a gutter, don't put so much waterproof cement on it that you create a dam that prevents water from flowing to the downpipe.

TIP

☑ To let water flow easier and to keep leaves and other debris in the gutter trough (and out of the downpipe, where it can clog), buy either a metal mesh screen that fits inside the hole of a downpipe or over the entire gutter trough itself.

REPLACING A WINDOW PANE

The biggest pain when it comes to replacing a window pane in an old wood window is that you have to install it from the outside. If you live more than two storeys off the ground it isn't always so easy: you'll either have to rent some climbing gear and suspend from your roof or figure out how to remove the entire window sash from the frame and bring it inside. That said, in most instances, you should be able to tackle the job without the help of a pro.

You will need	**HOW TO**
new pane of glass, measured to fit the window opening	**1** Put on leather gloves and remove any broken glass from the window sash.
leather gloves	**2** Scrape off any old glazing putty with a stiff putty knife or chisel and remove old glazing sprigs – the small triangular-shaped pieces of metal that stick in the wood sash – with pliers.
putty knife	
chisel	
pliers	**3** Sand the window sash smooth and paint on a coat of primer.
fine-grit sandpaper	**4** After the primer has dried, take the putty knife and apply a thin layer of putty to the window sash to act as a bed for the new glass (see Fig. A).
oil-based primer paint	
paintbrush	**5** Put the new piece of glass in place and push it gently into the putty. To secure it in place, push in new glazing sprigs with a chisel, 5cm (2in) from each corner and 15cm (6in) apart.
glazing putty	
glazing sprigs	

continued on next page

continued

6 Scoop out some glazing putty with your hands and roll it into a thin rope. Press this around the perimeter of the glass with your fingers to cover the glazing sprigs and seal the glass to the sash (see Fig. B).

7 Smooth out the glazing putty with a putty knife so that you end up with a neat, triangular bead of putty around the entire window.

8 After allowing the putty to dry for a week to 10 days, paint the glazing to match the colour of the exterior sash.

TIP

✓ When you paint new glazing putty, overlap the paint on to the glass to create a watertight seal between the window and the putty. Then, when the paint dries, use a razor blade to scrape the glass clean of extra paint and putty.

Fig. A

Fig. B

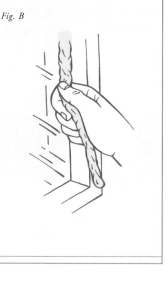

PAINTING A HOUSE

Painting is one of those things that isn't difficult to do but will make a huge difference to the way your house looks. But if you think all you have to do is open a tin of paint and start slathering it on the wall with a nice new paintbrush, think again. Most of the job is prep work – sanding, scraping, washing and filling nail holes. The painting takes up hardly any time at all.

You will need	**H O W T O**
dust sheets	1 Cover shrubbery and flower beds with dust sheets, and trim shrubs or trees so they won't brush against the house after the paint goes on.
bristle brush	
bleach	2 Remove birdhouses, light fixtures, house numbers and any other thing that might get in the way of the painting.
water	
scraper	3 Give the exterior of the house a good clean. Make sure you get under windowsills and any other hard-to-reach spots.
various-grit sandpaper	
dry cotton rags	4 If mildew is discolouring any unpainted wood-work, mix a solution of one part bleach to three parts water and scrub the area with a brush. Rinse with regular water.
hammer	
nail punch	5 Locate any painted woodwork that's blistered, peeling or cracking. Scrape or sand the area, then wipe it with a damp rag.
masonry filler	
putty knife	
oil-based primer	
ladder	
	continued on next page

continued

oil-based or cement paint

3.5 and 6cm (1½ and 2½ in) paintbrushes

small paint bucket with liner

bucket ladder hook to secure paint on the upper rungs

stirring stick

masking tape

6   Go around the house and set nails below the surface of any wood with a nail punch. After setting a nail, fill it with masonry filler. Once this has dried, sand it with a fine-grade sandpaper.

7   Prime all bare wood on the exterior of the house and let the primer dry overnight.

8   Start painting from the top of the house down: set a ladder to reach the eaves of the roof.

9   Then paint the woodwork, again from the roof down. Always paint windows from the inside out: first the sash (which holds the glass), then the sides, top, and bottom of the window, then the outer moulding.

DO'S AND DON'TS

✓   Always make sure your ladder is on firm ground and not on top of a dust sheet, a rock or a branch.

✓   Before opening a can of paint, shake it well, and then when you do open it, give it a good stir.

HINT

✓   Wet paint left to dry in direct sun will blister so paint west-facing walls in the morning and east-facing walls in the afternoon.

FIXING A SAGGING GATE

When they get old, garden gates can sag and get out of shape so that they won't close properly. The solution here is simply to replace rotten wood and the hinges and to add a turnbuckle to get the gate back in square.

You will need	**WHAT TO DO**
screwdriver	**1** Check the hinges to make sure the screws haven't started to come loose as a result of the constant opening and closing action of the gate.
wooden dowels	
wood glue	**2** If you see loose screws, tighten them. If the screws won't tighten because the holes are rotten or stripped, remove the screws and the hinge completely.
hammer	
wood screws	**3** Cut wooden dowels to fit the holes, put wood glue around each dowel and push into each hole, using a hammer if need be (see Fig. A).
new hinges	
turnbuckle	**4** Put the hinge back in place and drive screws into the holes and the new wooden dowels.
	5 If the gate has loose or slightly rotten mortise-and-tenon joints – where the tapered end of one piece of wood (the tenon) slides into a chiselled-out hole in another piece of wood (the mortise) – use screws and small wooden shims or wedges to secure the mortise in place.
	6 Place wedges on the top and bottom of the tenon along with a good amount of wood glue before pushing the wedges and the tenon back into the mortise (see Fig. B).
	continued on next page

continued

7 Then drive screws into the tenon and through the face of the wood into which the mortise is cut (see Fig. C).

8 If joints and hinges are solid but the gate is still sagging, attach one end of a turnbuckle to one corner and the other end to the opposite corner.

9 Screw the turnbuckle tight until the bottom of the gate comes into level (see Fig. D).

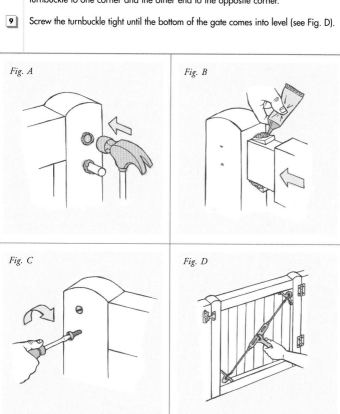

Fig. A

Fig. B

Fig. C

Fig. D

REPOINTING BRICK WALLS

Bricks are tough but they can get dirty and the mortar that holds them together can crumble. Like anything else outside your house, brick walls need to be cleaned and old mortar has to be replaced – a process called repointing.

You will need	**H O W T O**
hammer	**1** Rake out old and crumbling mortar with a hammer and chisel.
chisel	
brick mortar	**2** Mix up the mortar in a bucket. Scoop mortar on to a brick trowel, spread in place and use a pointing trowel to push the mortar into the gaps between the bricks.
small bucket	
brick trowel	
pointing trowel	**3** When enough mortar has been pushed in, dip an old paintbrush in water and rub it gently on the brick and the mortar joint to compact the mortar even more.
large, old paint-brush	
hydrochloric acid	**4** Let the mortar dry for half an hour, then use the tuck pointer to slice off any excess, so making the mortar flush with the brick.
water	
long-handled stiff-bristled brush	**5** Allow the mortar to dry overnight, then mix a cleaning solution of one part hydrochloric acid and ten parts water in a bucket.
	6 Dip a long-handled, stiff-bristled brush in the solution and scrub the brick and joint. This should clean the brick of any film or grime left over from the repointing.

CLEARING THE GARDEN

Garden work is an excellent excuse to get out of the house, clear your mind and get your hands dirty. It's also a great way to make your house look its best. A garden cluttered with leaves, stumps, fallen branches and debris is not going to impress anyone.

You will need	WHAT TO DO
leather work gloves **bin bags** **rake** **shovel** **old dustpan and brush** **electric chain saw** **secateurs** **pickaxe (for those with stumps)** **scrubbing brush**	**1** Put on your leather gloves and trim back overgrown shrubs and errant branches with secateurs or an electric chain saw, putting the branches in a neat pile near your work area. **2** Clear leaves and small branches from the lawn with a rake and an old dustpan. Put the debris in a bin bag and leave out for the dustman. If you have a compost, leaves are a great addition. **3** Small stumps don't look great and getting rid of them is hard but manly work. Use a shovel or a pickaxe to dig a deep trench around the stump. Then use a chain saw to cut the stump off about a 30cm (12in) below the surface of the garden. This only works if the tree is thoroughly dead. **4** Remove dirt and clean stone patios or concrete walks and driveways with a stiff scrubbing brush and water.

YOUR HOME

IS YOUR

CASTLE

A man's home is his castle because that's where he keeps all his stuff (in a well mannered, organized way, of course). He can invite friends over to play. Dates can admire things. Family can judge his income. Should all that stuff somehow disappear, however – say in a robbery or a fire – then a man's castle, whatever's left of it, doesn't amount to squat. That's why you need dogs, really scary ones. And good insurance.

GENERAL SECURITY

A good-looking, clean house where all your prized possessions are stacked neatly on shelves and in drawers can be a serene and enjoyable place to relax after a hard day's work. Unless, that is, someone breaks in and steals all your stuff. If that happens, not only will you not be able to relax but there's a good chance you'll be forced to miss the football on Saturday (because someone stole your TV). Here are some tips for keeping the thieves away and your stuff in place.

Make sure all doors and windows have secure locks installed on them. Each door should have both a dead-bolt (see page 136) and a chain lock. Front doors should also have "peep holes" so you can ID everyone that comes knocking.

Keep the outside of your house well lit. Garden lights work well and are stylish to boot. Motion lights that come on when someone is walking around the house are also effective at surprising anyone who isn't supposed to be there.

Plant prickly shrubbery underneath windows to make thieves think twice about venturing into the flower bed to access your home.

Keep valuables inside a fireproof safe well inside the house. Some crafty characters put two safes in the house – one as a decoy.

Avoid hiding keys in the obvious places such as under doormats and in flowerpots: most burglars aren't that dumb.

Get a burglar alarm. These things can be expensive but they can be set to alert the police department if a window or door is opened when you're not around.

CHOOSING THE RIGHT INSURANCE

Getting good home insurance is another key to keeping all your organized stuff safe (and all your handy repairs intact). Plus, should a mud slide, typhoon or some other natural calamity destroy the whole place, lock, stock and barrel, the right insurance can replace almost everything (including the roof and all your CDs). But beware: insurance companies have a bad reputation for being greedy bureaucratic liars and cheats. So make sure you read the fine print.

WHAT TO LOOK FOR

1. Before you sign on the dotted line, find out exactly what your insurance covers. Some cover just the structure and nothing inside (that's not what you want). Others might cover only the things that you list.

2. Make sure you're insured for enough money to replace all your stuff as well as the cost of rebuilding your house should the place get levelled by fire, flood, tornado or whatever.

3. Take an inventory of everything you own and its monetary value and keep that list, along with any receipts you might have, in a fireproof safe or in a safe-deposit box. If you do have to replace things, the insurance company may very well ask for just this type of thing.

4. Burglar alarms, good door locks, smoke alarms and fire extinguishers can lower your monthly payment.

5. The cost of insurance will go up if you smoke (you could, in theory, fall asleep with a lit ciggie in your hand and set the bedspread on fire). So either quit or tell the insurance company you don't smoke.

MAN'S BEST FRIEND: GUARD DOGS

When you lose your job and your girlfriend in the same week, there may be a few friends you can call to get drunk with but only one will be there to lick your toes: your dog. Canine companions also make for good security systems should you choose not to install an expensive high-tech alarm or plant prickly shrubs under the windows.

Of course you have to know which dogs will actually do something should an intruder stumble in through the window. Some dogs are all bark and no bite (these Fidos are known as watchdogs rather than guard dogs because they sound the alarm but that's about it) while other dogs will bark and then back it up with teeth, claws and muscle. Then there are dogs who won't do so much as lift an eyelid in the middle of the night no matter who walks through the door, including you.

The best watchdogs (barkers)	*The best guard dogs (biters)*
Yorkshire or Scottish terrier	**Doberman pinscher**
Miniature pinscher	**Mastiff**
Schnauzer	**Rottweiler**
Dachshund	**German shepherd**
	Not great barkers or biters
	Basset hound
	Bloodhound
	Bulldog
	Pug

SECURE WINDOWS

Without doubt, the weakest areas of a house are its windows, where panes can be broken as quickly as it takes someone to wrap his or her hand in a coat and smash it through the glass. Of course, this invariably makes a lot of noise, so most burglars would rather jemmy the lock. Either way, there are a number of methods for securing your windows before someone breaks in and swipes the power tools.

W H A T   T O   D O

1. The most practical way to ensure that your windows are secure is to have them all fitted with working locks and to make sure that they are always locked at night and when you leave the house.

2. For extra security on a double-hung window you can drill a downward-slanting hole through both window frames and insert an easily removable long nail or metal dowel.

3. A cheaper way to reinforce window locks is to put an old broom handle, cut in half, snugly between the top of the window and the casing above so that the window cannot be lifted without removing the broom handle from the inside.

4. Investigate the different types of extra-strength glass you can install in a window, all of which make it very hard to break. They include tempered glass, which has been heated at high temperatures and then cooled very quickly, forming a strong skin around the glass, and laminated glass, which is made by sandwiching a tinted plastic sheet between two panes of glass.

5. If you don't mind the occasional feeling that you're inside a prison cell, install iron security bars on the outside of windows.

6. Roll-down shutters also serve as good burglar deterrents, but unless you're living in a shop, you're going to look more than a little paranoid.

SECURE DOORS

Having a heavy, solid, wood front door with one bolt lock and one key-only dead-bolt lock will stop anyone from getting in. Here's how to install a dead bolt if you don't already have one. Make sure you buy a lock with the longest bolt possible.

You will need	**H O W T O**
tape measure	**1** Measure up 15cm (6in) above the doorknob or above the latch bolt on your door and make a pencil mark. Use a square to draw a straight line through this mark. This line will run through the middle of the circle needed to hold the dead bolt.
pencil	
square	
boring jig	
dead-bolt kit with bolt, template, face plate, striker plate and lock	**2** Place your template on the door. It should fit on the edge of the door, folding over from front to back. Line up the mark from step one with the corresponding mark on the template and use a pencil to transfer the reference points from the template to the door. These will show you where each hole needs to be drilled, including the one on the edge of the door where the bolt itself will go (see Fig. A).
drill with 22mm (7/8 in) spade bit and a 5.5cm (2 1/8 in) hole saw	
chisel	**3** Use a drill outfitted with a 5.5cm (2 1/2 in) hole saw and bore out the main hole in the face of the door. Before the saw passes all the way through the door, stop drilling and finish the hole by sawing from the other side.
hammer	
black shoe polish	
	continued on next page

continued

4 Change the hole saw for the 22mm (^{7}/8 in) spade bit and drill into the edge of the door to create a hole for the bolt to go through.

5 Put the bolt in the hole and position the face plate over it, in order to trace its outline on the edge of the door. Then chisel out the edge of the door so that the face plate will be flush with the wood once it is screwed in place (see Fig. B).

6 Fit the dead bolt together and secure it in place with screws. Screw on the face plate.

7 Dab the end of the bolt with black shoe polish, close the door and open the bolt into the door frame, leaving a black mark. This will determine where to drill for the dead bolt in the door frame.

8 Repeat step 5, this time with the strike plate, tracing its outline and chiselling the door frame out so that the strike plate will be flush with the wood. Screw the strike plate into place.

DO'S AND DON'TS

X Don't press too hard when you're drilling into a door or you'll splinter the wood. Just let the drill do the work for you.

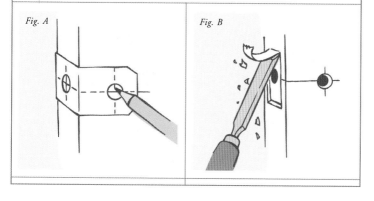

Fig. A

Fig. B

PREVENTING A FIRE
IN THE HOME

Even though you may get to show off your heroic side by saving your mother-in-law and your wife's parakeet from a crispy end, having your house catch fire is not cool. Not only will you have a load of blackened, charred wood to replace, but all that house cleaning and organizing you've just done will have been a complete waste of time. It's best to take some preventative action before it comes to that.

WHAT TO DO

1. Keep at least one fire extinguisher on every floor of the house and definitely one in the kitchen, where many fires start.

2. Smoke alarms can warn you of a fire before it gets out of control: install one in each room, near the doorway, and at the top of a staircase if you have one.

3. Keep rubbish, cardboard boxes, old clothing or any other combustible material at least 1m (3ft) away from furnaces and water heaters.

4. Check that your appliances don't have frayed electrical cords and if they do, fix them right away (see Chapter 2).

5. Keep plants and trees away from candles and heaters during Christmas festivities.

6. Keep candles at least 1m (3ft) away from curtains and always place them in some kind of ceramic or metal holder.

7. Never smoke anything in bed.

8. Check, or have a pro check, chimneys and fireplace flues regularly to make sure there is no crumbling mortar or cracking brickwork through which a flame could pass.

FIRE-ESCAPE PLAN

You might have done everything you could to prevent a fire but there is no legislating for Uncle Fred lighting up his Cohiba during nap time. Now the curtains are ablaze, the fire extinguisher is empty and the light fittings are starting to melt. What you need is a fire-escape plan.

You will need	**WHAT TO DO**
sheet of graph paper	1. To create an escape plan, draw the layout of your house, room by room, on a sheet of graph paper. Make sure you mark the locations of each window and door, and label the rooms.
pencil	
clear plastic folder	2. Write the word "EXIT" in capital letters next to each door that leads to the outside.
drawing pins	3. Draw small circles to mark the locations of every smoke alarm in the house.
	4. Walk through the house to determine which escape routes would be the fastest in case of fire. Draw arrows on your layout of the house, showing the route each person should take to get to an exit.
	5. Determine an outdoor meeting place – the neighbour's house, the corner shop – somewhere away from the fire, where you can all assemble for a head count.
	6. Make sure everyone in the house knows what the plan is by walking through the escape routes and by putting the marked-up graph paper in a clear plastic sheaf and pinning or taping it to an obvious place in the house, like near the back door or on the refrigerator.

HOLIDAY PRECAUTIONS

If you're going on holiday, you don't want your house to be taken over by wandering bands of gypsies who might come inside, sleep on the furniture and drink all your beer. To keep that from happening make it look like you never left.

W H A T   T O   D O

1. Leave a car parked in the driveway instead of the garage.

2. Ask a neighbour to collect your post and take in the milk in your absence (if you haven't cancelled it already).

3. Leave one or two lights on as well as the front-porch light. (A better option is to buy and install light timers, which allow you to have certain lights turn on and off throughout the day and night.)

4. Mow the lawn and rake any leaves just before you leave. Then arrange for someone to come over to mow and rake again while you're gone.

5. Leave a house key with your neighbour, along with an emergency phone number (of a good friend or relative that lives near by).

6. To save money on electricity and gas bills, adjust the heating thermostat and make sure all the lights are switched off.

7. Turn down the hot-water heater. There's no need to keep a tank full of water hot while you're gone. Then, if gypsies do break in, at least they'll have to take cold showers.

D O ' S   A N D   D O N ' T S

[X] Don't turn the heating all the way off if you'll be gone in super-cold weather, or the water in your plumbing pipes might freeze.

INDEX